Three Comedy Sketches

Michael Kilgarriff

Samuel French – London
New York – Sydney – Toronto – Hollywood

CONTENTS

By the same author

It Gives Me Great Pleasure (Handbook for the Music Hall Chairman)
Make 'Em Roar (two volumes)
Comic Speeches For All Occasions
The Golden Age of Melodrama

Compilations

1,000 Jokes For Kids of All Ages
1,000 More Jokes for Kids
The Musical Joke Book
Best Legal Jokes
Best Showbiz Jokes
Best Boss & Worker Jokes
Best Teenager Jokes
Best Service Jokes
Best Foreigner Jokes
More Best Religious Jokes
Even More Best Irish Jokes

Plays

Three Melodramas
Three More Melodramas
Music Hall Miscellany
Humpty-Dumpty in Nursery-Rhyme Land

PREFACE

When *The Heir's Return!* was submitted to Samuel French Ltd, that estimable firm kindly agreed to publish on condition that I wrote at least one other companion piece — and preferably two; thus encouraged I attacked the typewriter to see whether it would disgorge anything worthwhile.

In the mid-60s, I was engaged as musical director for a season of Old Time Music Hall in Ipswich; the programme included a mime version of *The Shooting of Dan McGrew*. Would this do? I re-read Robert Service's marvellous poem but thought it too dramatic, even tragic, for the purposes of an extended parody. And there was a further objection: since Service only died in 1958 his work was still in copyright. But the idea of a sketch set in the old Wild West seemed worth pursuing and so, reinforced by dim memories of an item in an old Hollywood musical, I struggled with the chosen rhyme scheme of *The Code of the West*.

It was while reading the lyrics of *I've Got the Ooperzootic*, famously sung by Johnny Danvers (Dan Leno's uncle) that my long-held ambition to write a sketch with an all-female cast began to come to the boil. The song made great play of the then novel — and to Victorian minds vastly comic — phenomenon of lady doctors. Would this offer sufficient grounds for humour to modern audiences? Not on its own, I decided. But if I were to add a villainess, a plot of labyrinthine complexity and a plethora of Gilbertian coincidences the resulting mix might prove acceptable. After protracted wrestling with storyline and construction *The Day of Reckoning* emerged.

For the initial production of *The Heir's Return!* I was careful to ensure that the artistes playing Mr and Mrs D'Arcy Hilliard were well established in the programme before appearing in the sketch, thus offering three levels of appreciation for our audiences to savour: the artistes themselves, Mr and Mrs D'Arcy Hilliard, and overlaying both the characters of Muriel and Aubrey Despard.

I was extremely fortunate in securing two excellent performers for this first production — my old friend George Little who brought immense energy and attack as well as some thirty years' experience as a professional actor to bear upon Mr Hilliard, and Aline Mowat, who so triumphantly surmounted the difficulties of playing Mrs Hilliard.

These two roles are by no means what are often described as actor-proof; D'Arcy can so easily be slow and ponderous, while the major problem with Eulalia is to show the gradations of her progressive intoxication. Drunkenness in women is not generally regarded as intrinsically funny, and it needs the lightness and delicacy of touch which Aline Mowat brought to the part to engage and retain an audience's sympathy. She never lost her charm or her femininity, nor did George Little lose D'Arcy's essential dignity — there must be finesse and integrity in the playing so that more is offered than a mere "send-up".

To Aline and to George, to our eminent musical director Grant Hossack, and to Pat Scott, the redoubtable wardrobe mistress of the Aba Daba company, under whose auspices *The Heir's Return!* was first produced, who made, mended and where necessary faked the costumes, my affection and grateful thanks.

Moreover, it was Miss Scott who, when I returned to the Aba Daba some months later to produce *The Code of the West*, made such an estimable Miss Jenny. Nor would the production have been possible without the unstinting co-operation of Paul Smith, who not only played the piano for the earlier parts of the programme but appeared on stage as Big Boss Kincaid. I must also thank Larry Barnes for providing so many of the Western properties and costumes as well as for making a truly impressive and sinister Big Dick. I was also lucky in having in my cast the enchanting Helen Watson, the riotously funny Michael Kirk, and Patricia Michael, the distinguished West End musical comedy artiste, who played Nell, Jack Pitt, and the Mayor (!) respectively. (Further details of the first performance are given in Author's Memoir on page 42.) To all of these friends and colleagues I again offer my heartfelt gratitude for putting their time, talents and reputations at my disposal.

Until a chance meeting in, of all places, Bexhill-on-Sea, I had not seen Liz York for no fewer than twenty-four years. While mulling over old times and catching up on each other's lives Liz told me that she ran an ILEA-funded amateur drama group. On my offering *The Day of Reckoning* for a try-out she very kindly found me a splendid director in Tim Webster, an enthusiastic cast, and most importantly of all, audiences for three performances. The first showing at the lively Gemini Theatre Company's own premises in Maida Vale, London, was successful beyond my expectations, the audience response more than compensating for all the headaches and reams of discarded paper which the writing of the sketch had incurred. For permitting me access to her company with all its considerable resources in youth and enthusiasm, Liz has my sincerest appreciation.

Michael Kilgarriff
Ealing, November 1982

THE HEIR'S RETURN!

NOTES TO THE PRODUCER

Appropriately enough it was an episode in the memoirs of the great Vesta Tilley—"The Irving of the Halls" as she was known in the United States—which provided the genesis of *The Heir's Return!* Dramatic interludes of very similar type, with the same repetitive dialogue, mindless patriotism and fatuous plot were staple items of Music Hall fare from the West End of London to the smallest market town. Herbert Tree, Ellen Terry, George Alexander and Sarah Bernhardt were some of the illustrious names from the legitimate stage who did not disdain the Halls—so enormous were the pecuniary advantages—although leading players of the time as well as lesser luminaries like the "D'Arcy Hilliards" always strove to maintain their superiority in the theatrical hierarchy.

Technically speaking dramatic pieces were only permissible in playhouses licensed for the purpose, and legal obstacles to their performance in Music Halls remained on the statute book almost until the Great War. These objections were commonly circumvented by the device of adding constant musical accompaniment and the inclusion of a song or two, thus instantly converting a play into what was known as a "burletta", a vague species of entertainment never adequately defined in law but hallowed by custom and practice.

It was while assembling and arranging the music for *The Heir's Return!* that I came across a song whose lyrics precisely echoed in tone, if not in content, the sentiments of my Soldier, my Sailor and my Chelsea Pensioner, and which showed me I was on the right track. This was *The Old Brigade*, composed by Odoardi Barri and written by none other than the egregious Fred E. Weatherly, who was responsible, among some fifteen hundred other perpetrations, for the lyrics to *Roses of Picardy*, *The Holy City*, and, most execrably of all, *Danny Boy*. But old Fred had his finger firmly on the pulse of the time, and if my dialogue was anything like his lyrics then I knew I must be making the right approach. I decided finally not to use the song other than as background to the appearance of the Chelsea Pensioner, for by the time he makes his entrance the sketch is well advanced and I felt that the denouement should be reached as quickly as possible.

The hackneyed construction of the piece is now so out of fashion that its very ridiculousness strikes modern audiences as divertingly authentic; so *The Heir's Return!* is a burlesque — but only just so. There is no villain — itself a pleasing novelty — but the sweetly ingenuous Muriel Despard was a stock figure of the era and the three twopence-coloured characterizations of Aubrey Despard were also much in vogue — Victorians liked their acting obvious and full-blooded; the understated "behaving" of Arthur Bourchier and Gerald du Maurier was to enchant a future generation.

Not that subtlety was entirely lacking (Irving was noted for the exquisite refinement of his playing) but in large auditoria with ill-lit stages, noisy audiences, bad sightlines and poor acoustics a degree of over-emphasis was essential if the dialogue was to be readily comprehended. There should therefore be a distinct difference in the playing of the preamble, that is to say from the arrival of the Hilliards in the auditorium until they exeunt to prepare themselves, and the sketch proper. The object is to establish the Hilliards so that the audience may learn a little about them: that D'Arcy comports himself with an unquenchable optimism allied to a seedy grandeur, that he adores Eulalia, that she has a weakness for the bottle, and that both are broke. The performances should be as naturalistic as the situation allows in order to contrast effectively with the "acting" to come.

It helps for the Chairman to produce the HOORAY!/NO! sign at the very start of the show during his warm-up, e.g. "Here we are, ladies and gentlemen, in the centre, nay the very heart, of the greatest Empire the world has ever known! (*He shows HOORAY! sign*) . . . Are we downhearted? . . . (*He turns it over to display NO!*) . . . Oh, well done! . . . I like a literate audience . . . that was in the nature of a rehearsal, ladies and gentlemen, for an item which you shall see later on in our programme. Never fear, when the time comes I shall reveal all . . . well, nearly all . . ." This will establish the sign, its use and the response expected.

If there is a long centre aisle it might be better for the Hilliards to enter from the side of the auditorium, through the pass-door, perhaps.

The Chairman can have a genuine script on his table DL to assist him with his cueing. He is, by the way, always scrupulously polite to the Hilliards, playing their game with an air of irony which should never descend to sarcasm.

If desired the table, the chair and the cardboard box can be brought on at the Chairman's signal by a comic stage-hand; he can be chirpy and enthusiastic or surly and disgruntled, and he constantly trips over an imaginary object on the stage at about LC — until his last exit after setting the cardboard box, when he finally manages to avoid this mysterious invisible obstruction and promptly falls over or bangs into something else.

Again if desired Mr Hilliard can have a dresser to help with his changes, although George Little managed by himself in a space the size of a telephone box! He played Hilliard as the eternal romantic, oblivious (except for a moment of exasperation on "*Still, madam . . .?*") of his wife's increasing incapacity, of his own mediocrity and of the patient unsuitability of the props and scenery (if any) supplied.

Back in the dear dead days beyond recall poor old D'Arcy (wherever did he dream up that name?) might have possessed a spark or two of genuine talent. Given better luck he might even have become a minor star, and though deep down he is surely aware that he has become an incorrigible second-rater he has written this piece as a vehicle for himself and is determined to give the audience the thrill of their lives. The actor must eschew any attempts at pathos, however. D'Arcy is far too resilient and vigorous for anyone to feel sorry for him, and he is still far too much in love with his beloved calling ever to feel sorry for himself. He may be disappointed at the inadequacy of his surroundings, and the props provided but as he says — "three boards and a passion, sir, is the essence of the drama. All else is superfluity and distraction."

George Little brought unbounded energy to the role; he relished hugely such words as *chariot* and *rigorous*, and his repetition of *h'old* throughout rang like a sonorous bell. Although he is a Yorkshireman we decided to keep Aubrey's three impersonations broadly (and phonily) Cockney, especially as Aline Mowat was playing Eulalia/Muriel in a Scottish accent — of which more anon.

We were careful to differentiate the Army salute from the Navy salute (the former with palm facing front, the latter with the palm facing down); at one performance on his line as the Chelsea Pensioner "Oh yes, 'e 'as " George managed to elicit the response of

"Oh no, 'e 'asn't!" from a particularly lively house. I am not in favour of rehearsed claques; such groups tend to shout their responses too loudly and too pat, and are obvious plants. Let your audience feel that they are making a genuine contribution to the fun; if you place the sketch in the middle of the programme (preferably immediately prior to an interval) they should be already participating in full measure. The whole question of Music Hall production and the problems of "taking the Chair" are dealt with in my book *It Gives Me Great Pleasure* (Samuel French).

The temptation to play the Chelsea Pensioner slowly must be resisted. After the appearances of the Soldier and the Sailor the general tenor of his utterances will be easily anticipated, and after the "sensational" revelation ("There have been no three servicemen here today—but only one!") the final few lines, often known as the "clean-up", should go at breakneck speed, with Mrs Hilliard going ape with the combination of gin and relief that her night's work is done.

Mr Hilliard is of course the more physically demanding role, but Eulalia/Muriel is perhaps the more difficult to play. The degree of expertise that Aline Mowat brought to the role can be gauged by the huge laugh—and often a round of applause—that greeted her first long speech ("By no means, Mr Hilliard . . . *hoi polloi*"). Also her increasingly incoherent renderings of "Thank you very much" were miracles of comic timing.

Mrs Hilliard has not the dedication to her art that her husband so manifestly possesses; one may imagine that she was never especially stage-struck nor especially gifted. I see her in her youth as a pretty empty-headed flibbertigibbet who drifted into a provincial chorus-line where her sexiness and ebullience caught the eye of an intense and earnest young actor. His looks and seriousness of purpose captivated her, and they married. But there were, alas, no children, her husband's career did not prosper and she took to the bottle. She still has the vestige of her early attractiveness and her youthful vivacity has not entirely deserted her. Whether her lack of talent and unprofessional behaviour have ruined her husband's career we don't really know, but he would be the last person on earth to blame her—for two reasons: firstly he worships her still, and secondly he would never accept that he *wasn't* successful. As is so often the way she is less naïve, and gin helps to take the edge of reality off the grinding poverty and squalor of their little world. He lives in

Fantasy-land, a citizen of Oz, but she can only follow him down the yellow-brick road by clutching firmly to her Gordon's.

Eulalia is also a touch coquettish — when she falls into a lap in the audience it is invariably a man's, and when she addresses the Chairman as "dear boy" she gives his cheek a playful squeeze. If the geography of the hall permits she can even dally with the pianist — I had the piano on-stage DR to facilitate this by-play. But she, like her gown, has seen younger days and her flirting is not pursued with much conviction — it is merely a reflex action, one feels.

Aline Mowat happens to be Scottish, and so gave Mrs Hilliard/Miss Despard a Kelvinside accent which gradually slid eastwards along Sauchiehall Street as the sketch and her alcohol intake progressed. Any accent with which your actress feels at home may be used, substituting dialect words for such expressions as "Ah me!" and "How wondrous!"

Mrs Hilliard's first speech as Muriel is vitally important and her tipsiness must not obscure the plot points — especially the codicil to her father's will concerning the missing cousin, Aubrey.

The repetitiveness of each sequence makes the dialogue difficult to learn and the musical accompaniment can be disconcerting to the players at first, so allow plenty of rehearsal time and get your pianist along as soon as the "books are down".

A touch of period flavour can be given to your programmes or songsheets by billing this sketch as follows:

THE HEIR'S RETURN!

by

Mr D'Arcy Hilliard

Cast of Characters:

Muriel Despard	Mrs D'Arcy Hilliard
An Old Soldier	Mr D'Arcy Hilliard
An Old Sailor	Mr D'Arcy Hilliard
A Chelsea Pensioner	Mr D'Arcy Hilliard
Aubrey Despard	Mr D'Arcy Hilliard

This billing will be too lengthy for your posters, of course, which can simply feature the sketch as:

!!!The Dramatic Sensation Of The Reign!!!

THE HEIR'S RETURN!

In One Apocalyptic Scene!

By Mr D'Arcy Hilliard

The four songs mentioned in the text, *Home Sweet Home*, *Soldiers of the Queen*, *Sons of the Sea* and *The Old Brigade* are all obtainable from sheet-music shops or from EMI Music Publishing, 138–140 Charing Cross Road, London WC2H 0LD. The lines quoted in this play from *Soldiers of the Queen* and *Sons of the Sea* are reproduced by kind permission of EMI Music Publishing Ltd.

THE HEIR'S RETURN!

The Heir's Return! was first performed at *The Pindar of Wakefield*, Gray's Inn Road, London on 13th May, 1982, with the following cast:

Chairman	Michael Kilgarriff
Mr D'Arcy Hilliard	George Little
Mrs D'Arcy Hilliard	Aline Mowat
Musical Director	Grant Hossack

Directed by Michael Kilgarriff

Scene: A Music Hall stage

Characters

Mr D'Arcy Hilliard: A grand old actor who relishes the mystery and the glory that he fondly imagines his profession represents; he might have made a good actor had his luck been better and he not been trammelled by his wife. He adores her, however, and is blind to her shortcomings, both personal and professional. He is in his early fifties, distinguished-looking and not without a natural dignity—the poor man's Irving.

Mrs D'Arcy Hilliard: One of the shabby genteel, without her husband's talent or dedication. She is a little younger than her earnest husband—or perhaps a great deal older; whatever her age, her face and figure are by no means ideal casting for "a young innocent maiden . . ."

Musical Director: Cheerfully insolent, but unmalicious.

Running time: 17 minutes

THE HEIR'S RETURN!

The Chairman's table and chair are DL, *and there are steps up to the stage from the auditorium*

Chairman Ladies and gentlemen, we were to have been honoured tonight by the personal appearances of those two ornaments of the British Theatre, Mr and Mrs D'Arcy Hilliard, who as you see from your programmes are engaged to present their celebrated one-act sensation, penned by Mr D'Arcy Hilliard himself, and entitled *The Heir's Return!* Well now, the properties for this distinguished representation have been delivered, but we are still awaiting the arrival of Mr and Mrs D'Arcy Hilliard themselves. I regret therefore that in the unforeseen event of their absence, we shall have perforce to continue with—

The House Lights fade up

Mr D'Arcy Hilliard enters through the auditorium down the centre aisle, carrying a silver-topped cane

Mr Hilliard Chairman! We are come!
Chairman I'm so relieved . . .
Mr Hilliard As I am, I can assure you, sir.
Chairman And your good lady?

Mrs D'Arcy Hilliard follows on behind her husband, enveloped in a large cloak or coat

Mrs Hilliard Yes, I'm relieved as well . . . (*Can it be that the eminent actress is a touch inebriated? Perish the thought! But endeavouring to rush after her husband she falls with a squeal into the lap of a male member of the audience*) Ooops! Sorry, dear!

Her husband goes and helps her to her feet and propels her in front of him

He's pickled! (*This refers to the man in the audience whose lap she has just vacated*)
Mr Hilliard Come, my cherub, our public is waiting!

*He and the Chairman assist Mrs Hilliard on to the stage with
whatever ad-libbing is necessary*

Chairman Perhaps you would care to rest? (*He leads her to his chair*
DL)

Mrs Hilliard Thank you, dear boy. (*She sits and leans sleepily on his
table*)

Mr Hilliard (*standing* C) Our profoundest apologies, sir, for this
tardiness — Tillings Omnibuses are so unreliable nowadays.

Chairman (*moving to his* L) Not at all, Mr Hilliard. We had
hoped — feared that you would not arrive at all. I take it you do
not possess your own conveyance?

Mr Hilliard (*astounded by the very suggestion, but recovering quickly
and playing along*) Hmmm? Oh, er — not just at the present . . .
our chariot is undergoing essential repairs. Occasioned by the
rigours of provincial touring, you understand.

Chairman Of course.

Mr Hilliard (*calling across*) Not that we complain about that, do
we, my petal?

Mrs Hilliard (*rousing from her torpor*) By no means, Mr Hilliard.
'Tis so gratifying to bring some uplift——

*She throws back her cloak revealing a massive bust, to which the
Chairman reacts, startled*

— to the lower orders . . . oh, yes, to bear the oriflamme of our art
to the masses . . . to shine a little cultural light into the gloomy,
tedious and boring lives of the *hoi polloi*. (*A degree of intoxication
is definitely discernible in the good lady's diction — the "h" of "hoi
polloi" seems, for instance, to give her a little trouble. Having
delivered this speech, her eyes glaze, and she falls delicately asleep,
her head supported on her left hand with her left elbow on the
Chairman's table*)

Chairman Quite so . . . I take it that Mrs Hilliard's deeply sensitive
(*looking at her then back to Mr Hilliard*) artistic temperament
was in some measure responsible for your delayed arrival . . .?

Mr Hilliard Er, well, in truth, Mr Chairman, in order to restore
her after the fatigue of the journey — from (*local unsalubrious
area*)——

*Mr Hilliard shudders at its mention and the Chairman grimaces in
sympathy*

—and to bolster her for tonight's ordeal we did have recourse to a neighbouring hostelry for a swift livener or two. (*He mimes drinking*) Just a stoup of mead . . .

The Chairman looks at Mrs Hilliard and she gives a loud hiccup

Chairman Or two . . .

Mr Hilliard Leaving me a trifle short . . . you couldn't, I suppose . . .? (*He bends his left hand backwards, palm up, as though soliciting for a tip*)

Chairman I'm afraid . . .

Mr Hilliard (*unabashed*) No, no, I quite understand . . . Well, now! (*He rubs his hands together*) To our buttons! Our properties are arrived?

Chairman They are, sir, and have been disposed according to your instructions.

Mr Hilliard (*moving* DR) Excellent—I do admire a well-conducted house. The setting calls for the richly appointed withdrawing-room of a noble English pile.

The Chairman indicates the bare stage apologetically with an undertone of irony. If practical he can give a sign to the stage-manager off-stage, at which runners can open displaying an exceedingly tatty and unsuitable back-cloth—a crudely painted panto-type cottage interior, for instance

Chairman This is the best we can offer, sir.

Mr Hilliard I see . . . yes . . . (*Disappointed but rising bravely above it*) Still, it's better than last week in (*again local unsalubrious area*).

Mrs Hilliard (*suddenly rousing*) Anything's better than last week in (*local*) . . . (*She instantly returns to her slumbers*)

Mr Hilliard And the intricately inlaid Adam occasional table?

Chairman (*fetching from* L *wing a scruffy card-table, opening it and setting it* C *with a noisy flourish*) This is as far as our resources will run, sir.

Mr Hilliard I see . . . and the elegantly carved Chippendale chair?

Chairman (*fetching from* L *wing a rickety folding chair, opening it and setting it at* L *of the table*) Here, sir.

Mr Hilliard I see . . . and the black japanned family deed box?

Chairman (*fetching from* L *wing a large battered cardboard box on* *the front of which is written in large letters EX-LAX and setting it on the table*) Will this serve, sir?

Mr Hilliard Hmmm ... 'twill no doubt see us through ... No matter—three boards and a passion, sir, is the essence of the drama. All else is superfluity and distraction. (*He moves* C) You have your sign? And your cues?

Chairman (*taking from the box a few scruffy handwritten sheets of paper and a large sign with HOORAY! on one side and NO! on the other*) I have, sir.

Mr Hilliard Good, good! A regrettable necessity but I have found some audiences of late a little slow to appreciate the nobility of the sentiments we endeavour to portray. Would you believe that on one occasion recently my wife actually received a raspberry on her entrance?

Chairman As opposed to the usual big hand?

Mr Hilliard Precisely. Now, sir—may I instruct your musical director?

Chairman By all means.

Mr Hilliard (*moving to wherever the Pianist happens to be*) Good evening, maestro. (*Grandly*) I am—D'Arcy Hilliard!

Pianist Wotcher, cock! (*Or local equivalent*)

Mr Hilliard (*disconcerted but quickly recovering his poise, drawing a crumpled, torn and stained piece of manuscript paper from his pocket*) Here is the musical accompaniment to our little offering, sir. It is marked "*Da Capo Al Fine*". (*This said exquisitely and with strong Italian accent*)

Pianist (*unimpressed*) From the top. Righto, cock.

Mr Hilliard again blenches at the familiarity and lack of respect. He returns to the Chairman's right. Both are standing below the table C

Mr Hilliard Is the fellow sound?

Chairman Maestro (*name*) is a very experienced musician, sir. He has been under some of the finest conductors in Europe.

Mr Hilliard That does not entirely surprise me ... (*crossing to Mrs Hilliard*) And now, my dear, if you are recovered ... (*gently shaking her shoulder*) ... Eulalia, my dove!

Mrs Hilliard (*rousing confusedly*) Strange that Nellie never writes ...

Mr Hilliard (*fondly*) No, no, my little pomegranate, not *The Woman Always Pays*. One of her early triumphs ...

Chairman (*moving above the table*) I remember it well. (*He grimaces*)

Mr Hilliard (*leading his wife to the* UL *entrance*) Come, my avocado pear . . .

Mrs Hilliard (*vaguely*) Where's the stage and what's the play?

Mrs Hilliard exits

Mr Hilliard *The Heir's Return!*, my sugar plum . . . what a woman! (*He turns out front dramatically*) Ha! I feel the Muse hovering . . . (*He strides to* DC) The readiness is all . . . how I long to give me Lear . . . (*Moving to* UR *entrance*) No matter . . . pray announce us, Mr Chairman. The game's afoot!

Mr Hilliard exits UR

The House Lights fade down. The Chairman moves to his table DL

Chairman Ladies and gentlemen, (*reading the script he has taken from the box*) rest assured that to all true devotees of the drama the miniature masterpiece you are about to see offers a great threat . . . (*he looks at the script again*) . . . treat. I ask therefore for your most earnest attention for (*he bangs the gavel*) *The Heir's Return!* (*Still looking intently at the script he holds up the sign displaying NO!*)

Mrs Hilliard enters UL *to shouts from the audience of "NO!" Naturally disconcerted she retires* UL *in confusion*

The Chairman immediately realizes his error and throws a whispered apology towards the wing

Er . . . (*He bangs his gavel again*) *The Heir's Return!* (*He shows the HOORAY! sign*)

Mrs Hilliard enters UL *to cheers. She has discarded her coat or cloak and hat, showing a faded, shabby ballgown and a tinsel tiara askew on her dishevelled hair. She is carrying knitting in one hand and a knitting-bag in the other*

The piano plays "Home Sweet Home" under the following speech

Mrs Hilliard Ah me, how strange that my father should have died and left me heiress to one million pounds! (*She stands* L *of the table. She puts the knitting in the bag and we hear a suspicious clink*

of bottles) It seems but yesterday that he told me (*she puts the bag down between chair and table, and a loud clinking is heard*) I should find something to interest me in this old deed box . . . (*she moves to above the table*) . . . and now I find myself the possessor of all the wealth it contains—(*she shows obviously phoney prop money*) cash, (*she shows papers*) share certificates, and (*she shows toilet roll, reacts and drops it back in the box, picking out more papers*) bearer bonds (*she drops them*) to the value of one million pounds! (*Moving* DR) But there is a codicil (*pronounced "co-de-seal"*) to Father's will which frankly bothers me. In the event of the return of my long-lost cousin—Aubrey (*this said in a terribly posh accent*)—I am to share the money with him. Well, I am not avaricious (*just a little trouble with "avaricious" may be detected*), and if the poor fellow does return after all these years I shall willingly carry out my father's wishes. But now, as I am alone, all the servants being out, I think I shall count the money whilst I need fear no interruption.

She trips to above the table as we hear three loud stamps from UR. *The music stops*

(*Shading her eyes and looking off* L) Who is—(*swinging round unsteadily to look off* R)—who is there? Why, it's an old soldier. Enter, my good old soldier!

Mr Hilliard springs into view UR. *He has taken off his overcoat under which he is wearing a military jacket. His hat he has changed for a solar topi or military hat, but his trousers and shoes are unchanged. On his upper lip is a large moustache*

Mr Hilliard Yes, madam—a h'old soldier! (*He salutes splendidly*)

There is a chord from the piano. The Chairman holds up the HOORAY! sign. Music plays quietly under the dialogue—"The Soldiers of the Queen". Mr Hilliard moves DR. *Mrs Hilliard sits in the chair* L *of the table*

A *h'old* soldier indeed, but 'oo 'as a good word for the *h'old* soldier on 'is return? When Mother H'England h'is in danger, it is the *h'old* soldier 'oo is called upon to fight 'er battles in far-off lands. There, clasping the flag 'e loves, (*suiting the action to the word*) 'e gives blow for blow. (*Still clasping the imaginary flag in his left hand he fights the foe with an imaginary sword in his right, backing to* DL) And shall 'e surrender to a savage mob? Shall 'e? *Shall 'e?*

The Chairman holds up the NO! sign

(*Fighting forward again to* DR) One more 'eroic effort, and the savages disperse, leavin' a small but gallant band wounded (*he clutches his arm*) and desperate (*back of right hand to brow*) — but victorious! (*Right fist raised high*) Victorious once again for Mother H'England!

The Chairman holds up the HOORAY! sign

But — what awaits 'im on 'is return to the bos*oom* of 'is Mother Country?

The music changes to "Soldiers of the Queen" played in a minor key. Mr Hilliard crosses to L *of the table, masking Mrs Hilliard who reaches down to her knitting-bag, takes out a quarter bottle of gin, removes the top and drinks*

The Work'ouse——

The Chairman leads the audience in "Aaah"

— the H'Union! No, not the H'Union, for at the Work'ouse door 'e is parted from 'is dear old wife, which is *dis*-h'union. And so, madam —

He moves R *disclosing Mrs Hilliard having a furtive tipple. He moves back in front of her with his open left hand behind his back, into which Mrs Hilliard places the bottle. He puts it surreptitiously in his trousers pocket*

And so, madam, you see before you the victor, and none to do 'im justice!

There is a chord from the piano. Mr Hilliard marches off in a circle L *of the table to the* UR *exit, saluting on the last word*

> "Weeeee'll —
> Gladly point to h'ev'ry one,
> Of H'England's soldiers of the Queen!"

Mr Hilliard exits UR

The Chairman holds up the HOORAY! sign

Mrs Hilliard How interesting . . . (*her inflexion implies that it was anything but*) . . . and yet, (*rising*) how sad . . . what terrible tortures our soldiers endure, but if England were to call tomorrow (*moving* DR) they would face them all again! Ah me! 'Twill be a sad day when British grut and plick —

She stops, puzzled. The Chairman, who has been earnestly bending over the script, picks it up and turns in his chair towards her, ready to give a prompt if required. But Mrs D'A repeats, carefully

— when British *pluck* and *grit* . . . do not respond to the call for protection for her Women and Children. (*She mimes a small child*) Thank heaven that day will never come!

The Chairman holds up the HOORAY! sign

Thank you very much . . . but after this stranger's visit, I must proceed to work and count the money.

She moves to above the box when again we hear three stamps on the floor from UR

(*Shading her hand and looking off* L) But who — (*she swings round even more unsteadily*) — but who comes now? Why, a poor old sailor! Enter, my good old tar!

Mr Hilliard makes another springing entrance UR. *He has removed the military jacket revealing a sailor's blouse; his hat is now a naval one and his moustache has been changed for a huge and patently false ginger beard. His shoes and trousers have not changed, however — nor has his performance*

Mr Hilliard Yes, madam — a *h'old* sailor! (*He salutes*)

The Chairman holds up the HOORAY! sign. A chord from the piano. Music continues under dialogue — "Sons Of The Sea". *Mr Hilliard moves* DR *in sailor-like fashion, hoisting his trousers fore and aft. Mrs Hilliard sits at the table*

A *h'old* sailor, h'indeed! When Mother H'England finds that she is being worsted in far-h'off climes, the Nelson spirit spurs 'im on. What cares 'e for h'obstacles? A dozen h'enemy ships face 'im? (*He mimes looking through a telescope*) 'E laughs! The raging seas threaten to capsize 'is ship? (*He mimes struggling with the wheel*) 'E laughs! 'Is dainty little wife is left weepin' on the shore? (*He points to tears trickling down his face*)

The Chairman encourages the audience to say "'E laughs!"

(*Indignantly—furious at the Chairman spoiling his moment of pathos*) No 'e don't—'e weeps!

The Chairman mouths a hurried apology and looks again at his script

(*Moving* DL *and attitudinizing heroically*) But the rum h'is served h'out, h'up goes the *h'old* H'Union Jack at the mizen, the guns spout forth, the *h'old* h'oak beams creak and 'e prepares to board the h'enemy ship. 'And to 'and they fight (*he fights back across to* DR), the foe is defeated, and the *h'old* sailor is carried back to *h'old* H'England with the *h'old* H'Union Jack flyin' from the mast-'ead of yet another prize!

The Chairman holds up the HOORAY! sign. The music changes to a minor key

(*Crossing to in front of Mrs Hilliard*) But—when 'e is too *h'old* to fight 'is country's battles, what does the h'old sailor get as 'is reward? H'Again the Work'ouse, the only 'ope for 'eroes. Still, madam—

He moves a pace L, *disclosing that Mrs Hilliard has taken a second bottle from her knitting-bag and is again fortifying herself*

Still, madam?

He moves back to mask her with his right hand behind his back, into which Mrs Hilliard puts the bottle

Till the voyage to 'is last resting-place 'e keeps 'is spirit 'igh—(*He dramatically raises his right hand, forgetting that it contains a quarter bottle of gin. Hurriedly he stuffs it in his trouser pocket*)— with a smile which is the h'only possession of h'every true-born Son of the Sea!

One bar lead in from the piano. Mr Hilliard with appropriate naval-type hauling actions, marches off to the last four lines of the chorus of "Sons of the Sea", ending with a salute on the last note. Unfortunately in his enthusiasm he marches in a cirle R *round the table to the exit* UL—*the wrong side*

"They may build their ships, my lads,
And think they know the game;
But they can't build boys of the bulldog breed,
Who made h'old H'England's name!"

Mr Hilliard exits UL

The Chairman holds up the HOORAY! sign

Mrs Hilliard How queer . . . (*rising with considerable difficulty — she is by now quite indisputably squiffy*) that today of all days two entire strangers should have invaded my privacy, (*moving* DR) and that these two men should——

Mr Hilliard creeps across behind her on tip-toe from UL *and exits* UR

Mrs Hilliard registers that something odd has happened, but doesn't know what

—have been members of the Army and the Navy, services of which England is justly pround. Gallant fellows, valiant and chilavrous . . . chisalvro . . . brave . . . no attempt to harm a defenceless young woman, or to take from her the fabulous sum entrusted to her charge. God bless them, I say, and send them safely home to their trusting womenfolk!

The Chairman shows the HOORAY! sign

Thank you very much . . . (*moving to above the table*) . . . but now I really must proceed with my work. I trust I shall not be interrupted again. (*She rummages around in the box, but no knock is heard. Swaying and glassy-eyed, she tries again*) I trust I shall not be interrupted again . . .

Mr Hilliard (*off*) Not ready—keep going!

Mrs Hilliard looks at the Chairman in anguish but he can only gesture helplessly. But like the true trooper she is she saves the situation by repeating her entire previous speech at breakneck speed. The Chairman frantically rustles his script trying to find out where she is

Mrs Hilliard Er . . . how queer that today of all days (*moving* DC) two entire strangers should have invaded my privacy and that these two men should have been members of the Army and the Navy, services of which England is justly proud. Gallant fellows, valiant and (*taking it very carefully this time*) chi-val-*rous*; (*she continues presto*) no attempt to harm a defenceless young woman or to take from her the fabulous sum entrusted to her charge. God bless them, say I, and send them safely home to their trusting womenfolk!

The Chairman shows the HOORAY! sign for a brief cheer

(*Out of breath*) Thanks ver' much . . . but now I *really must*
proceed with my work . . . (*moving to above the table*) . . . I trust I
shall be interrupted—I trust I shall *not* be interrupted again.

At last she hears three heavy stamps from UR

(*Beaming boozily with relief*) Did I hear a knock?

Again the three stamps are heard from UR

I *did*—I heard a knock! (*She looks off* R) Why, 'tis an old Chelsea
Pinsh'ner! Enter, my good old Chelsea Pinsh'ner!

Mr Hilliard enters UR *mightily afflicted with palsy and leaning
heavily on a stick. His sailor blouse is now covered with a
bemedalled Chelsea Pensioner's red coat, his hat is changed
appropriately, and his ginger beard has changed to a white chin-
beard. His trousers and shoes are the same—as is the character-
ization*

Mr Hilliard Yes, madam—a h'old Chelsea Pensioner!

*There is a chord from the piano. The Lights lower. The Chairman
holds up the HOORAY! sign. Under the dialogue is played "The Old
Brigade". Mr Hilliard lurches rheumatically* DS *and Mrs Hilliard
assists him to the chair* L *of the table. The chair should be pulled out so
that Mrs Hilliard has room to stand between Mr Hilliard and the
table. She leans on her table during the following speech, but standing
is too much for her by now, and she gradually subsides to her knees,
within easy reach of the knitting-bag which contains the third quarter
bottle of gin*

A h'old Chelsea Pensioner indeed! But beneath this garb there
beats an 'eart as brave as h'in the days of yore—and now?
Compelled to live on charity! A fittin' reward for years of battle
and deeds of bravery of which these medals speak . . . Yes, now—
what 'as 'e got? *Nuffin*! No 'ome, no comforts—*nuffin*! H'only the
knowledge of a task well done—apart from that, what 'as 'e got?

*The Chairman encourages the audience to say "Nuffin!!". Mr
Hilliard is furious again at one of his "points" being blunted. The
Chairman, who thought he was being helpful, looks confusedly at the
script*

Oh yes, 'e 'as—'e's got 'is pride! As 'e faces the final h'enemy,
Death, h'as gallant h'as the day 'e faced 'is country's foes!

The Chairman holds up the HOORAY! sign. The piano plays a bugle-call

(*Rising*) Charge!

*Mr Hilliard rushes palsiedly DR, uncovering Mrs Hilliard who has
retrieved the final bottle of gin from her knitting-bag and is drinking.
She realizes that Mr Hilliard has gone, heaves herself to her feet,
drops the bottle into the "deed-box" and lurches down to her
husband's side*

Pardon, madam, but I am *h'old* and weary, h'and the recollection
of my treatment by a h'ungrateful country h'overwhelms me . . .

Mrs Hilliard (*seizing him by the left wrist and pulling him none too
gently back to the chair at the table* L) You must rest your limbs,
my good old man. (*She plumps him down rather more firmly than
he would have liked and staggers DR*) Indeed, I know how valiant
and chilavr—(*she makes a gesture of disgust and mouths an
expletive*)—are the men of the Service. Why, even tonight I have
been visited by a Soldier and a Sailor. I, a defenceless young—
very young—maiden, yet no attempt was made to attack me or to
seize this great wealth (*indicating the box*), and now you arrive.
What can it all mean? Why do you make the third gallant man I
have met today?

There is a sustained tremolo chord from the piano

Mr Hilliard (*leaping to his feet and casting away his walking-
stick*) Madam—(*he throws his hat into the box and rips off his
beard, which also goes into the box*)—there have been no three
servicemen here today—but only one!

*He strikes a pose as a triumphant chord sounds, the Lights come up to
full and the Chairman shows the HOORAY! sign*

I came in disguise but to test you, and as I expected from one of
the Despards, I find in you all I have dreamed of in woman!
Honest, brave, and upright!

*Mrs Hilliard is standing stupefied, leaning on the table with her hand
in the box*

I greet you, and I kiss your hand!

A Chord. He pulls her hand out of the box and kisses it; Mrs Hilliard almost falls across the table

Mrs Hilliard (*pulling away and taking a step* R) How wondrous! 'Tis all clear to me now! (*With her right hand outstretched and index finger pointing skyward*) You must be my long-lost cousin! (*Her left hand is on her heart*)

Mr Hilliard (*taking a step* L) What use to deny it? (*Making the same gesture but with his left hand, his right hand being on his heart*) 'Tis I — Aubrey!

Chord. HOORAY! sign

Mrs Hilliard (*going to* R *of box and scooping out loose bank notes*) Then here are a million pounds which my father said I was to share with *you*! (*She skittishly throws them over him*)

Mr Hilliard (*having not changed his attitude*) Oh, happy day!

Mrs Hilliard Oh, rupture! (*She laughs almost hysterically*)

There is a swift piano intro during which Mr Hilliard grabs his wife's left wrist and pulls her C. *Both sing the following, with a simple one-two-three-hop dance to right and then to left*

Mr Hilliard }   Then let us be happy together,
Mrs Hilliard }   For where there's a will there's a way;
               Tomorrow the sun may be shining,
               Although it is cloudy today.

Mrs Hilliard tries another dance step but is pulled firmly back. Both stand close together clasping hands for the harmony

       Yes, tomorrow the sun may be shi — hi — hi — ning . . .

They do a final couple of dance steps on the last line which is in tempo

       Although it is cloudy today!

The Chairman shows the HOORAY! sign as both take bows extravagantly

Mrs Hilliard is blowing kisses to the pianist, and only reluctantly does she allow her husband to drag her off

Chairman Well, now, for those of you who would like to see that all again . . . (*he shows the NO! sign*) . . . I'm sure you'll be interested to learn that Mr and Mrs D'Arcy Hilliard will be performing *The Heir's Return!* for a most prestigious summer (*or whatever is the next season*) season—on the Goodwin Sands (*or local equivalent—marshland, sewage works, prison, etc. He then announces quite simply and straightforwardly*) The artistes involved in that farrago were of course your own . . . (*He gives their real names*)

FURNITURE AND PROPERTY LIST

If obtainable a back-cloth (behind runners if available) of any unsuitable scene, otherwise a bare stage.

On stage: Table DL
Chair DL
Steps up from auditorium

Off-stage L: Card-table **(Chairman)**
Folding chair **(Chairman)**
Large battered cardboard box marked EX-LAX. *In it:* cash, bearer bonds, share certificates, toilet roll, script, HOORAY!/NO! notice **(Chairman)**
Knitting-bag. *In it:* 3 quarter bottles of gin (empty!) **(Mrs Hilliard)**
Knitting needles and wool **(Mrs Hilliard)**

Off-stage R: Military hat, military moustache ready prepared with toupee tape for easy fixing and removal **(Mr Hilliard)**
Sailor's hat, ginger beard which can hook over the ears **(Mr Hilliard)**
Chelsea Pensioner hat, bemedalled coat, grey chin beard with toupee tape, walking-stick **(Mr Hilliard)**

Personal: **Chairman:** gavel
Mr Hilliard: silver-topped cane, tattered sheet of music manuscript in overcoat pocket

LIGHTING PLOT

A bare stage. Interior

To open: Bright general lighting

COSTUMES

Mrs D'Arcy Hilliard: Flowered Victorian/Edwardian hat, large overcoat or cloak, gloves. Faded ballgown (perhaps a converted wedding-dress) with matching shoes. No gloves with this dress—too many props to handle. Cheap tiara (worn under the flowered hat) and gaudy dress jewellery.

Mr D'Arcy Hilliard: Slouch hat (or top hat). Long black overcoat trimmed with astrakhan and with a flower in the buttonhole. Black trousers, shoes and socks. Tattered gloves. Silk scarf. Optional extras for his first entrance are a pince-nez attached to the lapel of the overcoat and a silver-topped cane. Under the overcoat and concealed by the silk scarf he wears the military jacket, and under that is the sailor's blouse or a horizontally striped tee-shirt.

MAKE-UP

Mr D'Arcy Hilliard: None.

Mrs D'Arcy Hilliard: Overdone juvenile look—be careful not to appear grotesque or panto dame-like. False eyelashes.

THE HEIR'S RETURN.

Michael Kilgarriff.

MUSIC FOR ENDING OF SKETCH.

CUE: "…. AS GALLANT AS THE DAY 'E FACED 'IS COUNTRY'S FOES! (HOORAY!)

PRESTO.

CUE: … "WHY DO YOU MAKE THE THIRD GALLANT MAN I HAVE MET TO-DAY?"

"MADAM — "THERE HAVE BEEN NO THREE SERVICEMEN HERE TO-DAY — BUT ONLY ONE!"

CUE: "I GREET YOU, AND I KISS YOUR HAND!"

"'TIS I, AUBREY!"

IN. 2

CUE: "OH HAPPY DAY!" "OH RUPTURE!"

THEN

F   D7

LET US BE HAP——PY TO-GE-THER.   FOR

G7   Am7   A#o   G7   V.S.

2.

WHERE THERE'S A WILL — THERE'S A WAY TO-

C7   F   Gmi   G#°   F

—MOR-ROW THE SUN — MAY BE SHIN-ING — , AL-

Bb   G7

COLLA VOCE

— THOUGH IT IS CLOU — DY TO — DAY. — YES, TO

G7   C7   F

TEMPO

—MOR-ROW THE SUN — MAY BE SH — I — I — NING —, AL —

TEMPO.

THOUGH IT IS CLOU — DY TO — DAY —

G7   C7   F

3

TABS.

PLAY AS NEEDED

4.

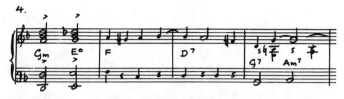

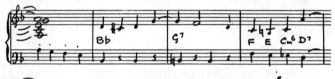

THE CODE OF THE WEST

NOTES TO THE PRODUCER

This mime piece is a broad, low-comedy burlesque designed for either a large or a small company and intended primarily, though by no means exclusively, for inclusion in an Old Time Music Hall production.

The characters involved are a narrator (the Poet), four named males and two females, with a further optional male role (the Shandy-Drinker) and any number of male and female extras, including an optional bar-tender. Obviously the numbers used and the resources available will materially affect any given production and so I have not attempted to give my usual comprehensive acting script. I have however given basic moves (note that in keeping with ancient theatrical tradition I have the goodies making their first entrances stage right and the baddies from stage left) and have indicated in these notes a general approach. More specific direction must be worked out in the study and in rehearsal according to the demands, talents and limitations of your company. In the text I have tilled the ground and sown the seeds; to reap the harvest you will have to employ your own ingenuity and imagination.

If you intend to play *The Code of the West* as part of an Old Time Music Hall, the narrator can be your Chairman. But he should not use an American accent which would cut across his persona as a superior middle-class Englishman. If you have a genuine American in your company he (or she) can recite the text from the stage on the side opposite the Chairman's table.

The lines should be spoken fairly swiftly, giving adequate pauses for the laughs, but taking the direct speech deliberately so that the characters "speaking" can mime their words accurately—and it is important that they should face out front while doing so. This synchronization produces a piquant effect which is vastly entertaining in its own right and should be given careful rehearsal. The speaker should also observe the metre and point up the rhymes; to facilitate this most of the comedy actions and reactions are placed at the end of lines rather than within them.

For the running gag on "the Code of the West" the action comes to an abrupt halt and the cast stand respectfully with heads bowed and hats and hands on hearts—except for Big Dick, of course, whose refusal to accept the Code underscores his evil nature.

Capital can be made from casting against type. For the first production my hero, Jack Pitt, who "walked tall and was tougher than any" was played by Michael Kirk, who is slight of build and possessed of wondrously comic mobile features; my Kincaid (Paul Smith) was tall, slim and manifestly far too young—his good looks by no means concealed beneath a huge walrus moustache and a pince-nez. My Mayor was the lovely Patricia Michael, wearing an absurdly phony false beard, a Churchillian bowler and a candy-striped suit, and my Miss Jenny, Miss Pat Scott, matronly of figure and mature in years, added to the bizarre casting. My Nell, however, was Helen Watson, whose face and figure were ideally suited to the role, and Big Dick was played by Larry Barnes, who while not especially big exuded menace and sexuality. Due to financial restrictions I had no crowd—but more about the first production later on.

The extra who fires the gun in the first stanza (causing everyone to start and glare at him) is also the Shandy-Drinker, another source of irritation to the others. So it is not surprising that he gets himself shot in the second stanza for a mere ten cents; he must be dragged out immediately or his body will be in the way for the subsequent action.

The crowd is on stage for the entire sketch and should not be permitted to distract from the principals. Your extras should be involved, concerned and energetic—but also disciplined; sometimes they will caper about and then freeze into sudden immobility, sometimes their movements will be violent and at others slow, dreamy and almost balletic. Style and precision are the aim, not just a gallimaufry of over-the-top romping. On the line "who could draw in a flash" they are all horrified at the prospect of Big Dick unholstering his pistol; but they show disgust and resentment when he fumbles the move—though only supernumeraries they want the sketch to be a big success and he has let them all down—and freeze immediately when he succeeds. They switch from observers to participators and back many times, and so must be clearly motivated and cleanly choreographed.

For the gun-shots use an off-stage nap-stick (two long flat pieces of wood hinged at one end and slapped sharply together).

Costumes can largely be improvized; if your production is for a modern revue casual clothes may be worn—the convention will be quickly accepted. The men must not wear wrist-watches which until World War I were worn only by women.

The only lighting cues are a cross-fade at the opening, a check down on the final stanza and black-outs for the last line and for the pictures. If you have a good board and plenty of equipment available (and a stage-manager who can attend sufficient rehearsals) you can make the lighting considerably more complex—isolating areas of the stage or individual characters, back-lighting the crowd, etc., etc. Make sure your narrator's face is well lit and that he or she is not just a disembodied voice emerging from the gloom by the proscenium arch.

Settings and furnishings should be simple and formalized—the only essential item is a chair for the Mayor (though if your auditorium has no rake it is as well for Miss Jenny to bring on a chair so that Nell can die sitting!). Personally I prefer any elaboration to be concentrated in the lighting, which if used imaginatively will help to sustain an allegorical style better than realistic scenery and props. True theatre is more concerned with creating an impression rather than presenting reality; we all experience the actual in our everyday lives so we go to the theatre to be offered enchantment—or at least a heightened semblance of the mundane. There is no reason why this sketch should not offer artistic integrity as well as belly laughs.

It can be advertised on your posters as:

A Fearsome and Frantic Frontier Farrago
THE CODE OF THE WEST
!!! In One Appalling Scene !!!

And in your programmes as:

The Dire & Dreadful Drama

THE CODE OF THE WEST

by

Michael Kilgarriff

Cast of characters:
The Poet
Nell
Big Boss Kincaid
Jack Pitt
Miss Jenny
The Mayor
Big Dick

Saloon Gals and Cowboys, Rustlers and City Slickers, Old-Timers and Injun Fighters, Sodbusters and 'Ornery Bushwhackers, Ramrods and Liquored-up Prospectors, Gamblin' Men and Carpetbaggers . . . Members of the (*name*) Company.

Scene: The Rotgut Saloon, Fate, Arizona
Time: Autumn, 1888

The musical accompaniment should punctuate the verse and the action rather than be continuous. I have included suggestions for specific tunes at various significant points but an experienced pianist will be able to extemporize without difficulty.

Author's Memoir

The special circumstances of the first production of *The Code of the West* are worth recalling if only to demonstrate how an idea can be developed and extended. Financial considerations prevailing at the time only permitted me a company of four — two female and two male, plus a pianist and a Chairman (myself). Since *The Code of the West* required two female and *four* male performers, where were the other two to come from?

I had been advised that the wardrobe mistress of the Aba Daba company who had been so helpful with the costuming of *The Heir's Return!* was an old variety hand; could she be persuaded to display her art in the interests of my sketch? Yes, she most certainly could. Now, Miss Scott did admit to me that she was in receipt of her retirement pension; her seniority of experience combined with an unusual generosity of both personality and vital statistics added an extra dimension to the role of Miss Jenny that I had not originally foreseen but which added very significantly to the success of the piece.

My pianist was Paul Smith. Prior to the production we had not met, but he came highly recommended as an excellent musician who in the past had shown his willingness to do rather more than was in the bond. When I outlined to him the nature of the engagement, his immediate reaction was, "Well, I'm game!" And thus was Big Boss Kincaid cast. But, you are wondering, if the pianist was playing Big Boss Kincaid, who was playing the piano accompaniment? The answer is that during the fourth stanza ("Though them varmints were mean their hands remained clean") I crossed over to Paul, whose piano was on stage, put a cowboy hat on his head and a large walrus moustache on his upper lip, ushered him into the action and then sat at the piano myself from where I both recited and accompanied.

Now for the Mayor: Miss Patricia Michael had up to that time played in no fewer than fourteen West End musicals, with starring roles in nine. Could she be persuaded to hide her remarkable beauty of face and form beneath a large ginger beard and a suit of male attire? Another telephone call elicited the happy information that this distinguished artist was also game.

The remarkable "Viceroy of Versatility" Larry Barnes, Music Hall buff and possessor of the largest repertoire of Music Hall songs in the business, lightning sketch artist, escapologist, ventriloquist, member of the Inner Magic Circle, honorary Pearly King and all-round good egg, consented to lend his talents to Big Dick; Michael Kirk, an experienced actor and Music Hall performer of small stature but large personality, agreed to essay Jack Pitt; and finally the petitely delicious Miss Helen Watson made the perfect Nell.

Nor must I omit to mention Mr Geoffrey Thomas, my friendly neighbourhood violinist, whose playing was of such assistance both for the sketch and for the song-scena which followed.

On the principle of what the eye doesn't see the heart doesn't grieve the lack of a crowd did not appear to lessen the impact of the sketch one whit; the novelty of the presentation, the eccentricities of the casting, and—dare I say?—the strength of the text were sufficient ingredients for success.

After the final black-out the lights came up to reveal Miss Jenny and Jack Pitt dancing to *Turkey in the Straw*, after which Miss Jenny exited leaving Jack Pitt to sing *The Camptown Races* with tambourine obbligato from Big Boss Kincaid. Nell, miraculously restored to life, entered to sing *Some Folks Do*, to be followed by Big Dick, ukulele in hand, who treated us to *Oh Susannah* with jug-band reprise (Nell on tambourine, Big Boss Kincaid on jug, Jack Pitt on jew's harp, myself on harmonica, and as mentioned above Geoff Thomas on fiddle).

Big Boss Kincaid continued with *Polly Wolly Doodle*, Nell with *My Blushing Rosie*, and Jack Pitt with that most ludicrously lugubrious of cowboy songs *When You Lay Me Six Feet Deep*, with parody choral accompaniment including Big Dick on guitar and again myself on harmonica. During all this Patricia Michael had changed from her Mayor's costume into something altogether more becoming in order to sing *Beautiful Dreamer*; Big Dick then started us all off on *Coming Round the Mountain* which heralded the entrance of Miss Jenny who interrupted with *Oh, Dem Golden Slippers*, and the entire show concluded with two further verses and choruses of *Coming Round the Mountain*—solo lines by Miss Jenny.

While not featured the cast sat on chairs upstage, minstrel-style; there were visual gags and all manner of novelties and surprises during this scena, which flowed naturally from the sketch and formed a very satisfactory and hugely popular sequence.

I had been so determinedly of the opinion that sketches belong in the middle of a Music Hall programme that I had planned for *The Code of the West* and the succeeding musical routine to occupy the centre section of the evening (at *The Pindar of Wakefield* there are always two intervals), but in the event the sketch and the scena as outlined above proved to be so strong that after the first performance I switched the second and third "halves" round in their entirety. This not only gave a better balance to the show but also gave my cast more time to establish themselves in the audience's affections before appearing in the sketch.

I have written in detail of this first production to show how seemingly insuperable difficulties can be turned to advantage; if after reading *The Code of the West* you consider that your company cannot provide the ideal cast, then consider what a less than ideal cast might achieve!

THE CODE OF THE WEST

The first performance of this sketch was given on 7th October, 1982, at *The Pindar of Wakefield*, King's Cross, London, for the Aba Daba Company with the following cast:

Chairman/Poet	Michael Kilgarriff
Nell	Helen Watson
Jack Pitt	Michael Kirk
Big Boss Kincaid	Paul Smith
Miss Jenny	Pat Scott
The Mayor of Fate	Patricia Michael
Big Dick	Larry Barnes

Directed by Michael Kilgarriff

Scene: The Rotgut Saloon, Fate, Arizona
Time: Autumn, 1888

Characters

Nell: A saloon girl with a shady past; a singer and dancer of sorts.
Jack Pitt: The hero, a ranch foreman.
Big Boss Kincaid: Jack's boss, a rich but honest man.
Miss Jenny: The heroine, Kincaid's daughter.
The Mayor of Fate: Greedy to get his hands on Kincaid's property—and his daughter.
Big Dick: Mean, moody and malevolent. The Mayor's hireling.

Running time: 10 minutes

THE CODE OF THE WEST

Chairman Ladies and gentlemen, I'd now like to prevent—present—a tale of the old Wild West. In this dramatic piece, the action takes place in the frontier town of Fate, a rip-roaring, rootin-tootin', wide-open, lawless kind of a place . . . rather like (*local*) on a Tuesday evening . . . though there was little respect for law and order in those parts they had their own ideas of what a man could do and what a man could not do: never shoot a man in the back, never kick a man when he's down, and never, never, draw on an unarmed man. These ethical principles . . . are now to be exhaustively explored in the piece you are about to witness, and entitled: *The Code of the West*!

Music plays "Oh Susannah" as the CURTAIN *rises. Cowboys and saloon girls are discovered posed. As the intro ends they are suddenly animated, dancing and roistering silently. If no curtains or runners available they can enter dancing. As the music ends the chorus all freeze as the Poet commences*

Poet

In the Fall of '88, in a town called Fate,	*Music recommences quietly*
A day's ride from the Rio Grande;	
Some cowpokes were hootin',	*Men mime dancing and shouting*
And gamblin',	*Mime card-dealing and dice-throwing*
and shootin',	*One man fires. All react crossly*
And drinking hard liquor,	*All men drink and put glasses down*
and shandy!	*Same man drinks. All react to him*
There the West it was wild,	*Same man is shot and dragged out,*

No place for a child;
Only men who for ten cents
   would shoot yer.
And women like Nell,
Who could sing like a bell,
A gal with a past, but no
   future.

In the Rotgut Saloon she
   would dance,
She would croon,

And many's the man who
   pursued 'er;
They'd shout and they'd
   holler,
They'd offer a dollar,

And their comments got
   louder,
And lewder!

Though them varmints were
   mean their hands remained
   clean,
Of foul murder and rapin' the
   women;
For of Big Boss Kincaid they
   were all plumb afraid,

And he didn't admire such
   sinnin'.

His young foreman, Jack Pitt,
   was a man of true grit,
With his fists the men knew
   he was handy;

to general approval

Killer is rewarded
*Nell enters UL. Music: "Oh,
   Dem Golden Slippers"*

Nell poses C seductively

Two bars of the Can-Can
*Nell opens her mouth but we
   hear a swanee whistle or
   duck-call*

She pushes one chancer away

They mime doing so briefly
*All wave notes but she gestures
   dismissively*

One "shouts" in her ear
*One other man whispers in her
   other ear*
Appalled, Nell slaps his face*
*   and exits UL in high dudgeon*
*The men look mean and then
   nod virtuously*

*Men all rise respectfully, as
   Big Boss Kincaid enters UR.
   Music: "Hail to the Chief"*
*Kincaid wags his finger. Men
   cower*

*Jack enters DR. Music:
   Fanfare*
*All nod admiringly as he
   shadow boxes*

* This could be the Poet/Chairman.

In the saddle for weeks,
They'd all split their breeks,
They were most of 'em sore,
  chapped and bandy.

He mimes riding
All men put hands to bottoms
All sit wincing. Jack walks
round bandy

Yes, Jack Pitt he was bluff,
Jack Pitt he was tough,

He poses—men applaud
silently and girls look
longingly

He walked tall

He tries to do so
unconvincingly

  and was tougher than any;

He turns suddenly frightening
men behind him

But what he knew best was
  the Code of the West,

All stand and bow heads with
hands and hats on hearts.
Chord

And he loved Kincaid's
  daughter, Miss Jenny.

Jenny enters DR. *Men adoring,*
women jealous. Music: "I
Dream Of Jeanie". Kincaid
nods approvingly

She was maidenly pure, and
  coyly demure,
Unlike Nell whose neckline
  made men quiver;

She simpers C. *Kincaid looks*
proud
Music: "Oh, Dem Golden
Slippers". Nell enters L *next*
to Jack, who gazes at her
bosom over her left shoulder,
quivering

Though while flaunting her
  charms,
Nell but longed for the arms,

Her right hand snakes round
his head

Of Jack—

Miss Jenny grabs him by the
right ear and pulls him
across her to where Kincaid
can take the ear and remove
Jack from temptation off-
stage R. *Miss Jenny then*
shoos Nell off L

—who'd no chance to
  deliver.

Now the Mayor of Fate was a
  man filled with hate,

"Villain" music. Lights can
flash if practicable. Mayor
enters L

Whose lusts and desires they
  were many;
His ambition no less was one
  day to possess,
Kincaid's cattle and ranch—
  —and Miss Jenny!

How he coveted that land,

And Miss Jenny's white hand,
So he hired Big Dick, a
  gunfighter;

Who could draw in a flash,
(*Meaningfully*) Who could
  draw *in a flash* . . .
And then have a slash—

  —with a *knife*!

At your face: what a blighter!

His roots were unknown but
  his fame it had grown,

And the Mayor had found
  him in Tucson (Too-son);
Where in a back bar he had
  caused a fracas,
By pleas'ring a gal with his
  boots on.

Big Dick had known Nell, but
  not very well,

He rubs hands and grins evilly

He looks off R
He looks off L

*Raises fists imploringly to
  heaven*
Kisses his own hand vicariously
*Music: Chopin's "Funeral
  March". Big Dick enters* UL
  chewing a cigar menacingly
Fumbles the draw. Crowd react
*"All right! All right!" Second
  attempt is successful*
*He turns upstage as though
  about to undo his flies, but
  turns to Poet with ?
  expression*
*"Oh . . ." Takes knife from
  back of belt and waves it
  threateningly at crowd or
  audience if there is no
  crowd. Wipes knife and
  replaces it in sheath*

*Swaggers about. Girls make up
  to him but he brushes them
  off*

They shake hands

Flicks cigar away
*Looks pleased with himself—
  polishes his nails on his
  leather waistcoat, perhaps.
  The Mayor exits* DL *shocked*

*Music: "Oh, Dem Golden
  Slippers" as Nell enters* L.

Way back East when he
    couldn't afford 'er;
Now he'd shoot in the back,
Boss Kincaid and young Jack,

Have a beer, and then Nell,

In that order!

He'd long hardened his breast
    to the Code of the West,

And Nell's troublesome
    conscience she stepped on;
From the clutches of Fate,
She just couldn't wait,
So she said she'd help Dick —

    — with his weapon!

In the Rotgut Saloon, Dick
    had filled a spittoon,

He was wild as a vengeful
    gorilla,
A-thirstin' for slaughter —
But just then Kincaid's
    daughter,
Came in for a swift
    sarsaparilla.

She stopped dead in her
    track —
Where was father? Or Jack?
But Dick had took a shine to
    her pretties;
Her frills and her lace,

*They see one another, react
and embrace*
Dick draws gun
*Mimes firing in two directions
then reholsters gun*
*Mimes taking glass and
drinking*
Grabs Nell on "order"

Breaks from her DR *and stands
with arms defiantly folded.
Chord*
*But she has a struggle to
subdue her better nature*
Looks round, trapped
Moves to Dick
*Holds her hand at his crotch
level*
*He slaps his gun into her hand
and she exits* L
*He paces about then spits. A
cow-bell is struck, attracting
all eyes to the pit or
wherever the sound has come
from*
*He continues pacing back and
forth*

*Music: "I Dream Of Jeanie".
Jenny enters* L

*Sees Big Dick and recognizes
trouble*

*She trembles under his lustful
gaze — but could it be that
she finds him perhaps a little
more exciting than her*

betrothed, young Jack Pitt?
He is circling round her, and
she is still like a hypnotized
rabbit

Her sweet innocent face,

She manages a flutter of the
eyelids

And specially the thrust of
her — ankles.

He is now just above her R
shoulder, leering at her bust

He was close by her side,
"What would you?" she cried;

Miming her line out front

He leered coarsely and winked
a red eye.

He does so

"My horse," he did say,

Miming the lines out front

"Has been hungry all day;
He wants his oats now — so do
I!"

He puckered his lips, ran his
hand round her hips,

She is perhaps not so distressed
at these familiarities as she
should be

As he seized her she
shuddered with dread;

Or does she shudder with
sensuality?

He was tasting that peach,

Kissing her on the right cheek

When a hard voice said,
"Reach!

Jack enters R

Ya galoot! Let her go, or taste
lead!"

Music: Fanfare. He points gun
at Dick

Yes, 'twas Jack to the aid of
the fair Miss Kincaid,

She runs to behind Jack

But as he drew a bead on
Dick's hide;

About to shoot

"I'm unarmed!" said Big
Dick,

Miming the words

As he raised his hands quick,

He does so

It was true — just for once he'd
not lied.

Dick is DLC, *Jack* DRC, *Miss*
Jenny URC

And young Jack passed the
test

He looks noble

Of the Code of the West,

For rules men must have to
  survive;
To the floor his gun fell,
Then Dick yelled "OK Nell!
Now slip me my Colt 45!"

What dastardly treachery!
Not to mention what lechery!

Dick's gun was concealed in
  Nell's gusset!
But now the time came for
  him to reclaim
His gun—she just wouldn't
  discuss it!

Dick or Jack? To which one
  should she give up the gun?
For the other would sure bite
  the dust.
When a shot filled the air:

'Twas the Mayor . . .

    . . . on the stair!

And Nell dropped with a slug
  in her bust!

Next Jack would have died
  but Kincaid was outside,
Just in time to prevent Jack's
  demise;
By drawing his pistol,

*All show respect except Dick.
  Chord*
*Jack looks at his gun and
  raises it*
Swanee whistle effect
*Miming the line. Music:
  Quick snatch of "Oh, Dem
  Golden Slippers" as Nell
  enters L, crossing Dick to C*

*Dick looks smug. Nell turns
  upstage and pulls gun out
  from under her skirt*
*Dick reaches for the gun but
  she hesitates*

*She looks at each
  indecisively—she cannot see
  Jack shot in cold blood*

*Mayor enters L with gun.
  Music*
*Gunshot. All turn and look at
  him. Jack raises his hands*
*Mayor looks bemused, then
  grabs a chair from off L and
  stands on it*
*Nell slides to the floor (or on
  to a chair placed in position
  by Miss Jenny)*

*Kincaid enters R to "Hail to
  the Chief"*
*Sees what is going on and
  reacts*
He does so

And sending an epistle,   *Aiming at the Mayor under*
    Jack's R *arm*

Of twenty-two calibre size!   *Gunshot*

Through the Mayor's ugly   *Swanee whistle, and again as*
  head,   *Mayor falls into the arms of*
Down he fell slightly dead;   *two men who carry him off.*
    Or he can be caught by Dick
    and Jack, who also bundle
    him off into the wings and
    then return

Dick would hang for his part   *Kincaid pulls Dick off* R *by the*
  in the quarrel;   *kerchief round his neck,*
    holding it like a noose.
    Chopin's "Funeral March"
    (1 bar)

And Miss Jenny would marry   *They meet* C *and hold hands.*
  her Jack,   *Quick burst of "I Dream of*
But let's tarry,   *Jeanie"*
At the Rotgut Saloon for the   *They part and move upstage to*
  moral: *Nell, Miss Jenny on her* R
    and Jack on her L

'Twas poor Nell who   *Lights lower. "Oh, Dem*
  expressed it,   *Golden Slippers" plays softly*
Although they had guessed it,   *in minor key. Jack is*
And she said as she went to   *supporting Nell's shoulders*
  her rest: *and Miss Jenny weeps into*
"I deserve now to croak,   *lace handkerchief*
For I went and broke,   *Mimes line*
The inviolable Code . . . of the   *She dies. Men remove hats.*
  West!"   *Major chord. Black-out or*
    curtain

1st picture: *Same lighting as for last stanza. Jenny and Jack stand*
              LC, *she weeping on his shoulder. Jack's hat is over Nell's*
              face. Black-out

2nd picture: *Full up. The entire company, goodies and baddies, and*
              even the Poet if not the Chairman, dance a square-dance
              to the music of "Turkey in the Straw", and the curtains

> *or runners come in. If no curtains or runners the*
> *company can dance off*

Chairman I'm sure you would all agree that that was a tragic
disaster of the first water . . . and speaking of water, I wish it was
the interval . . . (*Or if immediately prior to an interval*) . . . and
speaking of water, you'll be relieved to learn that the last time
we did this show, at about this point in the programme, we had
an interval, and it was such an enormous success that we
thought we'd have another one just like it tonight So let us all
reconvene in ten minutes or so. Thank you.

He bangs his gavel, blows out the candle and exits

The music reprises "Oh Susannah"

FURNITURE AND PROPERTY LIST

Back-cloth of the Rotgut Saloon with a bar UC. Otherwise just a bare stage—no doors or windows or treads; these will be too specific for the style of the sketch

On stage: Tables. *On them:* bottles, glasses, cards, dice
Chairs

Off-stage: Chair off L **(Mayor)**
Chair off R **(Jenny)** (*optional*)

Personal: **Male Crowd:** dollar bills, guns and holsters as available
Jack: gun in holster
Big Dick: cigar, knife in sheath, gun in holster
Mayor: gun
Kincaid: gun, pince-nez or steel-rimmed spectacles
Jenny: lace handkerchief
Female Crowd: handkerchiefs to cry into as **Nell** dies

LIGHTING PLOT

A Saloon. Interior

To open: Special on **Chairman**

Cue 1	**Chairman:** "*The Code of the West!*" *Cross-fade to* **Poet**; *bring up bright general lighting on saloon*	(Page 47)
Cue 2	**Poet:** ". . . at the Rotgut Saloon for the moral:" *Check down*	(Page 54)
Cue 3	**Nell** dies *Black-out*	(Page 54)
Cue 4	When ready for 1st picture *Bring up Lights to same level as Cue 2, then Black-out*	(Page 54)
Cue 5	When ready for 2nd picture *Bring up Lights to full*	(Page 54)

EFFECTS PLOT

Cue 1   **Poet:** ". . . and shootin'."   (Page 47)
Gunshot (nap-stick)

Cue 2   **Poet:** "There the West it was wild,"   (Page 47)
Gunshot

Cue 3   **Poet:** "She would croon."   (Page 48)
Swanee whistle

Cue 4   **Poet:** ". . . Dick had filled a spittoon,"   (Page 51)
Cow-bell

Cue 5   **Poet:** "To the floor his gun fell."   (Page 53)
Swanee whistle

Cue 6   **Poet:** "When a shot filled the air."   (Page 53)
Gunshot

Cue 7   **Poet:** "Of twenty-two calibre size!"   (Page 54)
Gunshot

Cue 8   **Poet:** "Through the Mayor's ugly head." (Page 54)
Swanee whistle; repeat as **Mayor** *falls dead*

COSTUMES

Poet: Evening dress, preferably in period.

Nell: Mae West ensemble, or bespangled leotard with fringe. Lots of feathers and flashy costume jewellery. Long gloves and black tights with garter on one thigh.

Miss Jenny: Poke bonnet, gingham dress with lace and frills, gloves. Falsies if necessary.

Jack: Cowboy outfit with white hat perhaps too large for him and baggy chaps.

Kincaid: Either cowboy outfit or period suit with bowler hat.

The Mayor: Black frock-coat and trousers, coloured waistcoat. Top hat. White shirt with black string tie. Watch chain. Dress rings.

Big Dick: Black cowboy outfit with black hat and black kerchief round neck.

Male Crowd: Western outfits, all with hats. Coloured check shirts, leather waistcoats, neckerchieves, chaps, etc.

Female Crowd: Similar to Nell but less striking. All tarty.

Bartender (optional character): Striped shirt, bow-tie, apron, arm-bands.

MAKE-UP

Poet: Straight.

Miss Jenny: Peaches and cream complexion. Dark hair with ringlets. No false eyelashes.

Nell: Heavily rouged, long false eyelashes. Piled-up hair.

Kincaid: Grey hair and moustache. Pince-nez or steel-rimmed spectacles.

Jack: Straight.

Mayor: Black eyebrows, black line under eyes. Possible black beard.

Big Dick: Tanned. Blue chin. Only he to have black moustache. Sideburns.

Male Crowd: Sideburns, tanned. Beards and unshaven chins.

Female Crowd: Like Nell, only less so.

COSTUMES

MAKE-UP

THE DAY OF RECKONING

NOTES TO THE PRODUCER

As I progressed with the initial drafting of *The Day of Reckoning* I began to realize that the sketch was turning into something rather different from the intended burlesque melodrama; what emerged, apart from the welter of coincidences with which the plot abounds, was a pastiche of the Christmas pantomime "sob" scene.

There are a number of these in the panto canon — Cinderella telling Buttons that she is not in love with him, Jack Trot informing his mother that he has sold Daisy the Cow for a mere bag of beans, Mother Goose bidding Priscilla to leave home — in which strong drama and comedy are interwoven and with pathos contiguous with bathos; there are tears through the laughter and laughter through the tears.

So this is the approach to be considered when tackling *The Day of Reckoning*; the performances should be broad but sincere and the emotions played for real, without clowning or over-forced mugging.

Mrs Goodheart might be thought of as an Old Mother Riley; she is very volatile and given to rapid and extreme changes of mood — she is also on-stage for the entire sketch and should therefore be given to an experienced player of proven staying-power. Her crying jags need careful orchestration and her hysterics graded, or her utterances will be tiresomely alike. For Mrs Fubbs I have imagined a lovable eccentric of the kind so superbly portrayed by the wonderful Irene Handl. Her catch-phrase, "Oo, I say!" occurs no fewer than eleven times, each of which must be clearly differentiated — surprise, dismay, disgust, fright, amazement, salacity, sympathy, astonishment, terror, revulsion, and delight — in that order.

Prudence is the "Principal Girl" in the Alice Fitzwarren/Goldilocks/Princess Aurora mould — roles which can so often be insipid but which can be enlivened by a sparky personality. She is overjoyed to be united at last with her elder sister, for whom she immediately develops a starry-eyed infatuation. Her movements should be neat and balletic. "Mama" and "Papa" have the accent on the second syllable.

Lady Audley is, of course, the villainess, a handsome, even beautiful woman who crumples quickly enough under Dr Probity's remorseless disclosure of her past and present infamous conduct. The more arrogant and contemptuous she seems prior to this the more satisfying is her come-uppance.

Dr Probity is the "Principal Boy" — Prince Charming, Dick Whittington, Robinson Crusoe and Robin Hood all rolled into one. She is brisk, efficient, lofty-minded and possesses considerable moral fibre; but she must also have great charm and femininity if she is not to become just a priggish cypher. Her expository speeches must be taken swiftly but clearly in ringing Heldentenor-like tones without being hoydenish. We must like Dr Probity as well as respect her. She shows the softer, gentler side of her nature by reciprocating Prudence's affection.

As in pantomime your players should aim most of their dialogue straight at the audience, only looking at other characters on stage when listening — and not always then. In my previous three books of sketches I have given this same instruction but I make no apology for reiterating it here for it is an essential element of melodrama technique. At first your company will find it strange and awkward, but persuade them to persevere and to be bold. Dr Probity especially tends to speak, as Queen Victoria complained of Mr Gladstone, as though addressing a public meeting, and lines like Lady Audley's sinister "he died quite recently . . . and quite suddenly . . ." will lose half their force if not directed straight over the floats.

Keep the moves clean-cut and definite; if you have a small stage you may prefer to eliminate some of my directions or they may appear fussy and give rise to masking problems.

Note that Mrs Goodheart and Mrs Fubbs always address Lady Audley as "me lady", the mode of address of an inferior, whereas college-educated Prudence insists on calling her simply "Lady Audley" as though a social equal — and naturally Dr Probity does the same.

I have written the two elder ladies as Cockneys; also all place names in the text are in the London region. If you wish to set the sketch in your own area Mrs Goodheart and Mrs Fubbs can have local accents and the place names altered to suit. Prudence, Dr Probity and Lady Audley should always have standard "received English" accents, again in conformity with panto tradition, though

Lady Audley's accent can slip a few notches down-market after her identity as Elsie Sproat is revealed.

The Day of Reckoning is, I feel, too long for non-stop musical accompaniment, but chords or "stings" should underline all significant moments during the action, and each character has a theme tune which should be used for each of her entrances. One important character who does not actually appear is Sir Trueman Probity; at each mention of his name *A Fine Old English Gentleman* might be played. I have indicated suggestions for each leitmotiv, though your musical director may have other ideas. All songs mentioned are obtainable from sheet-music shops or from EMI Music Publishing, 138–140 Charing Cross Road, London WC2H 0LD.

Your Chairman's or compère's introduction can be on the following lines:

"Which brings us, my lords, ladies and gentlemen (*or* The entire second half of our programme is devoted) to an intensely—not to say excessively—dramatic offering the like of which has not been seen since the discovery of chloroform ... yes, in *The Day of Reckoning* we give you (*holding up paper and then putting on spectacles*)—I just have to put my spectacles on to read this—my old house-master's warnings are coming home to roost ... yes, in *The Day of Reckoning* we give you laughter ... sin ... tears ... sin ... anger ... sin ... joy ... (*he looks at the audience expectantly*) ... oh, you are quick! (*He looks at the paper again and registers disgust*) ... purity?! ... (*now happy again*) ... and sin! Not bad for a Thursday night in Scunthorpe, is it? (*Alter to suit*) So we invite you now to cower in your seats as you witness that curious and conglomerate coagulation of coincidences, entitled *The Day of Reckoning!*" (*He bangs his gavel and exits*)

After the conclusion he can enter and say:

"Well, now, wasn't that—er—wasn't that something? I won't say what ... but did you follow the plot? ... More twists than a game of pontoon ..." (*He then announces the next item—see my "It Gives Me Great Pleasure"—or if an interval follows he can continue with:*) "But after that traumatic—dramatic experience I daresay we could all do with a breather, so let us all now stretch our legs and reassemble in fifteen minutes or so. Thank you." (*He bangs his*

*gavel, blows out the candle and exits. The band plays one chorus of,
say, "If It Wasn't For the Houses In Between"*)

The sketch can be billed on your posters as:

The Renowned Tragi-Comedy

THE DAY OF RECKONING

Virtue Triumphant! Vice Vanquished!

And in your programmes as:

The Programme will include that Devastating Divertissement
in one Soul-Searing Scene

THE DAY OF RECKONING

by

Michael Kilgarriff

Dramatis Personae:
Mrs Goodheart
Miss Prudence Goodheart
Mrs Fubbs
Lady Audley
Dr Probity

If desired this sketch can be extended to last for an entire middle
section of your programme (i.e. with an interval on either side) by
the insertion of songs—a device again well within the pantomime
and melodrama tradition. If anyone in your cast possesses a special
skill such as tap-dancing, juggling or playing a musical instrument
this talent can be pressed into service ("Let me cheer you up, Mama
dear/For see, I have my trumpet here!") The following suggestions
should add about twelve minutes to the running time, making some
forty minutes *in toto*. All these songs are obtainable from EMI
Music Publishing Ltd, 138–140 Charing Cross Road, London
WC2H 0LD, with the exception of *There'll Always Be an England*

which is published by Dash Music, Campbell Connelly, 37 Soho Square, London W1.

Skylark: To be sung by Prudence after her line "Poor Mama . . . poor Papa . . . poor Matilda . . ." (page 72). Alter lyrics to suit.

Call Round Any Old Time: To be sung by Prudence after Mrs Fubbs' exit (page 73). Prudence to extend her next line as follows: "Thank you, Mrs Fubbs . . . how considerate she is! We may be poor in material possessions but we are rich in neighbourliness. For what we say is . . ." She sings one chorus, repeating the last eight bars.

Never Mind: To be sung by Mrs Fubbs after her line ". . . ten years ago to this very day." (page 74). Instead of weeping she says, "Still, never mind, eh?" and sings one chorus solo, then a second joined by Mrs Goodheart and Prudence in harmony.

From Poverty Street to Golden Square: To be sung by Lady Audley. After her line ". . . and I'll distrain your miserable possessions into the bargain" (page 76) she adds "and then you'll find that—". She sings one chorus in sneering contempt, possibly repeating last sixteen bars. Then cut to "And now—Fubbs!"

Let the Rest of the World Go By: To be sung by Mrs Fubbs and Mrs Goodheart. After ". . . just you sit there and try not to fret, Mrs G" (page 78) Mrs Fubbs continues with "What if 'er ladyship *does* chuck you out? I'll tell you something for nothing—if she does, I'll come with you!" She then sings the first verse and chorus, Mrs Goodheart sings the second verse and they both sing a second chorus in harmony.

There'll Always Be an England: To be sung by Dr Probity. After speech ending ". . . none is more respected in the civilized world" and Mrs Fubbs' "Ear, ear " (page 79) cut Dr Probity taking Mrs Goodheart's pulse and Mrs G's line "But—". Instead Dr Probity sings a chorus and the first verse. On the second chorus a songsheet can be lowered from the flies, or alternatively the words can be given in the programme ("Come on everybody—number five!") and the House Lights raised.

A Boy's Best Friend Is His Mother: To be sung by Dr Probity after

"Mother!" (page 81). She sings one chorus (altering sexes to suit) and then repeats the second half with Prudence.

We All Came in the World with Nothing: To be sung by Mrs Goodheart. After "Yes, make a nice change, any'ow" (page 86) she continues with "But do you know . . .?" and then sings the first verse and chorus solo; everyone joins in a second chorus except Lady Audley who can sit sulking on the chair UL, her back to the audience. This chorus might also be on the programme, with the House Lights raised.

FINALE: After the final line ("And today is the Day of Reckoning") use either *Then Let Us Be Happy Together*, the finale song from *The Heir's Return!* on page 32, or reprise the chorus of *From Poverty Street to Golden Square*. Everyone dances round happily except Lady Audley who remains UC, scowling and sorting the washing. Finally Mrs Fubbs, of all people, feel compassion and drags her into the celebration, and Lady Audley succumbs to the general air of innocent happiness. This ending should be used instead of and not as well as the two pictures given on page 87.

THE DAY OF RECKONING

The first performance of this sketch was given by the Gemini Theatre Company at their headquarters, St Saviour's Church Hall, Warwick Avenue, London W9, on Saturday, 13th November, 1982, with the following cast:

Mrs Goodheart	Lorraine Duffy
Miss Prudence Goodheart	Jackie O'Leary
Mrs Fubbs	Margaret Bunce
Lady Audley	Caroline Draper
Dr Probity	Rita Fox

Directed by Tim Webster

Scene: Mrs Goodheart's kitchen, Battersea
Time: Early afternoon, Friday, 30th March, 1890

Characters

Mrs Eliza Goodheart: A sorely-tried and lachrymose woman of 50.
Miss Prudence Goodheart: Her daughter; pretty, kind, loyal, virtuous to the point of ostentation. An English rose of 20.
Mrs Phoebe Fubbs: Their neighbour; amiable and eccentric but a good friend. 51.
Lady Audley: Their landlady. An imperious, very striking-looking femme fatale. Rotten to the core. Mid-40s.
Dr Matilda Probity: Tall, strapping, liberated, with the keen intelligence and independent spirit much advocated and admired by Shaw. Not mannish but cool and competent. Very precise in speech and manner. 25.

Running time: 25 minutes

THE DAY OF RECKONING

The scene is the humble kitchen in Battersea, London, of Mrs Goodheart and her daughter, Prudence. There is a table slightly UC *with a chair at each downstage corner; there are entrances* L *and* R *with a chair below each*

As the CURTAIN *rises Mrs Goodheart enters* R, *staggering beneath the weight of a huge bundle of washing done up in a sheet. She lurches* DL *and then backs* UC, *depositing the bundle on the table. Music:* "*If It Wasn't For the Houses In Between*"

Mrs Goodheart (L *of the table*) Gawd strewth! I got to get all this washed and ironed and mended and darned by tea-time! That gives me——

A cracked bell strikes two

—two hours! (*Moving* DR) Still, if I get it done in time the Vicar's wife 'as promised me an extra 'halfpenny and a bowl of gruel, like the kind and generous lady she is! (*Moving across to* C) I'll share the gruel with Prudence, my daughter—no, I'll give 'er it all, for she needs to keep up 'er strength for 'er studies, the dear girl. (*Moving* DL) No takin' in washin' and gettin' red 'ands for 'er—she'll pass 'er exams and be a schoolteacher, or even a typewriter, maybe! (*Moving back to the table*) Yes, I'll see to it that she escapes from this 'orrible place or my name's not Eliza Good'eart—a widow . . . 'ow proud 'er father would 'ave been! (*She weeps and sits* L *of the table*)

Prudence enters, skipping in through R *entrance carrying books. Music:* "*O, Star of Eve*" *from* "*Tannhauser*"

Prudence Hello, Mama dear. I came in the back way because— why, you're crying!
Mrs Goodheart No, I'm not. (*But she has another spasm of sobbing*)
Prudence Oh, but you are! (*She puts the books on the table and stands* C) What's the matter?
Mrs Goodheart Don't you know what today is?

Prudence (*gaily*) Of course — it's Friday!

Mrs Goodheart (*with some asperity*) I know it's Friday! (*Tragically lachrymose again*) But it's also . . . (*she gulps with emotion*) . . . March the thirtieth!

Prudence Oh, of course — how could I forget? The anniversary of my father's accident.

Mrs Goodheart And of your elder sister's disappearance . . .

Prudence (*crossing to* L *of Mrs Goodheart and sitting at her feet*) Tell me about it again, Mama dear, if it won't upset you too much.

Mrs Goodheart Twenty-five years ago this very day, your father — oh, 'e was such a lovely, tall, 'andsome man, was my Charlie . . . always upstandin' . . . (*thoughtfully*) . . . yes . . . well, a lot of the time . . . anyway, 'e took our first-born, your elder sister Matilda, to 'Yde Park to see the gentry ridin' in Rotten Row. I can see them now, on that dreadful Sunday morning, 'im so proud and — upstandin' . . . oo, 'e was a right Charlie . . . and 'er, a golden-'aired little mite not quite a year old, sittin' on 'is shoulders, laughin' and prattlin' and piddli — dribblin' down 'is back collar-stud . . . out they went, through that very door—— (*She points* L *and stops, overcome by tears*)

Prudence (*continuing an oft-heard tale*) And three hours later Papa was brought home——

Mrs Goodheart (*nettled*) 'O's tellin' this story? (*She reverts to her mood of tender reminiscence*) And three hours later your father was brought 'ome on the back of a knacker's cart, all twisted, broken and bleedin' . . . 'e'd been run over by a carriage and pair in the Park . . . and as for your sister, Matilda, we never knew what 'appened to 'er, and we never saw 'er again! (*Rising*) Gorn! Gorn! And never called me Mother . . .! (*Sitting*) Any'ow, they put your father to bed, and 'e never rose again.

Prudence Never?

Mrs Goodheart Well, once or twice — 'e *was* your father . . . 'e languished in bed for ten long weary years and then . . . (*overcome again*) . . . and then . . . 'e snuffed it! (*She weeps*)

Prudence (*rising and crossing* DR) Poor Mama . . . poor Papa . . . poor Matilda!

Mrs Goodheart But now I must tell you about *my* elder sister, Phoebe.

Prudence (*turning in surprise*) I never knew I had an Aunt Phoebe!

Mrs Goodheart Maybe you 'aven't, not now. 'Cos the same thing 'appened to 'er! When I was only a little baby our father took 'er to see the fair on Clapham Common, and neither of 'em ever come back. The Peelers looked everywhere, but they never found 'ide nor 'air of 'im or of Phoebe. And that was fifty years ago to this very day—March the thirtieth!

Prudence (*to* C) What a curious coincidence! But let me do the washing for you, Mama dear. You shouldn't have to work so hard on this day of all days.

Mrs Goodheart (*rising*) No, Prudence, you go and get on with your studies.

Prudence (*taking her books and crossing to* L *entrance*) Very well, Mama dear.

Prudence exits L

Mrs Goodheart (*moving to above the table and sorting out washing*) March the thirtieth . . . 'ow I always dread this day . . . oh, me 'eart! . . . (*clasping each affected part and staggering to the chair* R *of the table*) . . . oh, me side! . . . oh, me back! . . . oh, me front! (*She collapses in the chair*)

Prudence enters L *and hurries to Mrs Goodheart's side*

Prudence Mama dear, what is it?

Mrs Fubbs enters R. *Music: "Ain't She Sweet?"*

Mrs Fubbs (*crossing to* DL) 'Ello, Pru. I just come to borrow a few bile beans, if you got any spare. I seem to be a bit out o' sorts, know what I mean? (*She cackles and turns*) Oo, I say! Is your mother took bad?

Prudence Yes, Mrs Fubbs. She's been working too hard again. To pay my college fees, you know.

Mrs Fubbs Yes, she's a good soul. (*She takes a small bottle of gin from her pocket*) She needs a drink . . . (*she proffers the bottle then changes her mind*) . . . of water. (*Crossing* DR) I'll go to the well and get 'er some.

Mrs Fubbs exits R *swigging from the bottle*

Prudence Thank you, Mrs Fubbs.

Mrs Goodheart (*faintly*) Charlie! Is that you, Charlie? (*She tries to rise*)

Prudence No, Mama dear, it's Prudence. Don't stir.

Mrs Goodheart I must, I must! (*She heaves herself to her feet and crosses to* L *of Prudence*) What about me washin'? The Vicar's wife promised me an extra 'alfpenny . . . (*at* L *of table sorting through washing*) . . . there's your fees . . . the rent . . . the tally-man . . . the burial club . . . oh dear . . . (*she sways and leans on the table*)

Mrs Fubbs enters R *with a cup*

Mrs Fubbs (*to Prudence*) 'Ere you are—Adam's ale, fresh drawn.

Prudence (*taking the cup and handing it to Mrs Goodheart*) Thank you, Mrs Fubbs, you're so kind. (*Gently handing Mrs Goodheart into the chair* L *of the table*) Drink, Mama dear, it'll make you feel better.

Mrs Goodheart drinks

Mrs Fubbs (*sitting* R *of the table*) Truth to tell, *I* woke up this morning feelin' a little dicky . . .

Prudence (*crossing* DL) Did you? I haven't been feeling myself lately, either . . .

Mrs Fubbs What a shame!

Mrs Goodheart (*putting the cup on the table with a clunk*) It's this slum we 'ave to live in! It's not fit for a pig! No light, no air—it's un'ealthy, that's what it is! Un'ealthy! (*In quiet desperation*) We got to get out of 'ere, Prudence, afore we're done for . . . like your late 'usband, Mrs Fubbs.

Mrs Fubbs You're right, Mrs Goodheart. Big strong man Fubbs was till we come 'ere. Then 'e just seemed to fade away like . . . 'ere! That was March the thirtieth—(*weeping*) ten years ago to this very day!

Prudence (*crossing to* C) Ah, what a dire anniversary March the thirtieth is, to be sure. On this day what calamitous, doleful events have befallen. You, Mrs Fubbs, lost your husband——

Mrs Fubbs weeps noisily

—you, Mama dear, lost your father and your elder sister——

Mrs Goodheart weeps loudly

—and I lost *my* father and *my* elder sister—— (*she also weeps*)

All —on this very day!!! (*All howl*)

Lady Audley enters L

Music.

Lady Audley And on this very day I'll have my rent!
Mrs Fubbs Oo, I say!

*Thunder. Lights flash. Music: Rachmaninov's "Prelude in C minor".
Mrs Goodheart and Mrs Fubbs rise respectfully*

Mrs Goodheart (*moving to Lady Audley*) Oh, me lady . . . just give
me a little more time to pay——
Lady Audley (*crossing DR*) Time waits for no man, Goodheart. Not
even—for me! I've come for my arrears, and I mean to have
them—*all*!
Mrs Goodheart It's only two years, me lady. 'Is lordship never
bothered us much——
Lady Audley The Marquis is dead!
All (*with identical gestures of surprise and dismay*) Oh, horror!
Lady Audley Which is why you see me in mourning . . . yes, he died
quite recently . . . and—quite suddenly . . . but *I* am not so easily
humbugged. Goodheart—the rent!
Mrs Goodheart Oh, me lady, I've not been well—me daughter's
college fees 'ave gone up, and——
Lady Audley Excuses, excuses! Sending this chit to college, are
you? What effrontery! Getting ideas above your station, aren't
you, Goodheart? (*She moves C and beckons Prudence to her side*)
Come here, girl.

Prudence obeys

Let me have a good look at you . . . (*she raises her lorgnette*) . . .
hmmm, bright eyes . . . soft skin . . . (*ingratiatingly*) Why don't
you come into service with me, my dear?

Mrs Fubbs moves to Mrs Goodheart

I need a new lady's maid . . . yes, you're really quite a pretty little
thing, aren't you? Under those dowdy clothes . . . (*she strokes
her*)

Prudence, mesmerized, shudders

Mrs Fubbs Oo, I say!
Mrs Goodheart (*crossing to between Prudence and Lady
Audley*) My Prudence in service? Never! I 'aven't scrimped and
slaved all these years to see 'er edication thrown away on bein' a
domestic!

Lady Audley (*crossing* DR) You stupid woman! What pathetic pretensions! I'm offering this girl a life of ease and luxury and you . . . (*she decides upon a new tack. She turns and moves back to Mrs Goodheart. Coaxingly*) I could cancel your arrears, Mrs Goodheart—and even reduce the rent in future. What do *you* say, my dear?

Prudence I must be obedient to my mother's wishes, Lady Audley.

Lady Audley Little fool! Very well! Wallow in your squalor! You have one hour—one hour in which to pay me in full! Otherwise it's out into (*local*) street with the pair of you . . . (*crossing to* L *entrance*) . . . *and* I'll distrain your miserable possessions into the bargain! Do I make myself plain?

Mrs Fubbs (*sotto voce. To Prudence*) Makin' 'erself very ugly, I'd say.

Mrs Goodheart Yes, me lady.

Lady Audley Good. And now . . . (*moving in and speaking sharply into Mrs Fubbs's left ear*) Fubbs!

Mrs Fubbs (*dithering*) Oh! . . . ah . . . mmm . . . er . . .

Lady Audley Don't be so feeble, Fubbs. According to my late husband's accounts you owe me—half a crown!

Mrs Fubbs (*edging across to* R *entrance*) Yes, me lady. I got it in me kitchen somewhere, I think.

Lady Audley (*following her*) I'll come with you to collect it. I don't want you skulking off.

Mrs Fubbs Yes, me lady . . . no, me lady . . . Oo, I say!

Mrs Fubbs exits R

Lady Audley Remember—one hour!

Lady Audley exits R

Crashing minor chords. Lightning and thunder

Mrs Goodheart Oh, Prudence, what are we going to do?

Prudence puts her arm comfortingly around her mother's shoulders

We're ruined! Me 'ome, me bits and pieces, me knicker-knacks, me furniture—all lost! Even the bed where your father and me . . .

Prudence moves away L *embarrassed*

. . . oh, 'e was such an upstandin' man . . . if only 'e was 'ere now! [Green Light]
If only . . . (*staring out front*)

Ghostly greenish lighting

Charlie! It's 'im! I can see 'im!

Prudence (*turning in alarm*) Mama!

Mrs Goodheart Charlie! 'Elp me! In the hour of me greatest trial—
'elp me! There, you see? 'E smiled! Everything's goin' to be all
right—I know it!

Prudence (*leading her to the chair* L *and standing on her left*) Mama
dear, please calm yourself!

Mrs Goodheart (*delirious*) Yes, everythin's goin' to be wonderful
. . . Charlie'll see to that, won't you, Charlie? Oh! (*She throws her
apron over her face and sits motionless*)

The lighting returns to normal

Mrs Fubbs enters R

Mrs Fubbs (*to* C) Well, that's seen Lady Muck orf for a bit—'ere!
Your mother gone doodle-alley again?

Prudence Yes, she has, Mrs Fubbs. Her mind's wandering! (*Crossing to Mrs Fubbs*) I really think I should fetch a doctor to her, but
we've nothing to pay a doctor with!

Mrs Fubbs Tell you what—why don't you pop over to Archie
Carter's at number five? 'Is missis is 'avin' 'er seventh and 'e told
me the doctor's with 'er now. It's a new doctor in these parts.
Archie said the name was . . . er . . . Probity. That was it—Dr
Probity!

Prudence Dr Probity? But he's famous!

Mrs Fubbs Is 'e? Oo, I say!

Prudence And a famous doctor wouldn't bother with humble folk
like us.

Mrs Fubbs Oh, I dunno. Archie Carter's only a Member of
Parliament and you couldn't get much 'umbler than that, could
you?

Prudence Very well, I'll do it! I'll throw myself on this doctor's
mercy and implore him to come. I'd do anything to save my dear
Mama's wits.

Mrs Fubbs Anything?

Prudence Anything!

Mrs Fubbs Oo, I say!

Prudence (*moving* L) Stay with her please — good, kind Mrs Fubbs!

Prudence exits L

Mrs Fubbs (*moving to Mrs Goodheart's right*) Now you cheer up, Mrs G. (*She takes the cup from the table and offers it to the motionless figure*) Go on — 'ave a drink of water . . . no? Well, I will . . . (*she takes a sip and pulls a face*) No, well, p'raps you're right. (*She puts the cup back on the table and sits R of the table*) Do you know, I give that stuck-up Lady 'Oity-Toity me 'alf-crown *and* I give her a tanner orf your rent an' all, and she flounces out of me kitchen without so much as a thank-you! And they say the gentry is always polite — well, I tell you somethin', Mrs G — I don't think she's proper gentry at all! There's somethin' about 'er that isn't quite——

Mrs Goodheart (*rousing suddenly and pulling down the apron*) Where's my daughter?

Mrs Fubbs (*rising and moving in to her*) Gone for the doctor. 'Ow're you feeling, dearie?

Mrs Goodheart Doctor? We've got no money for doctors! And what about me washin'? (*She tries to rise*)

Mrs Fubbs (*pushing her back into her seat*) Now you just sit there and try not to fret, Mrs G. Oo, I say — you do look done up!

Mrs Goodheart (*smiling wanly*) Do I?

Mrs Fubbs That's right! Try and look on the bright side.

Mrs Goodheart It's just that I have to smile whenever you say that, Mrs Fubbs.

Mrs Fubbs Say what, Mrs G?

Mrs Goodheart What you just said — "Oo, I say". My dear father always used to say that, or so me mother told me.

Mrs Fubbs (*sitting R of the table*) Did 'e? So did mine! Though that's about all I *can* remember of 'im. When I was just a nipper 'e took me to the fair on Clapham Common, and got 'isself run over by a h'ominibus. A number forty-two . . . 'ere! I've just realized! That was fifty years ago to this very day! Yes . . . March the thirtieth!

Mrs Goodheart Eh?

Mrs Fubbs Well, after 'e was run over 'e was far too gone to tell anybody 'oo 'e was or 'oo I was, so I was took to a h'orphaninidge. All I could tell 'em was me first name.

Mrs Goodheart (*trembling*) And what would that be, Mrs Fubbs?

Mrs Fubbs Me first name? Phoebe, why?

Mrs Goodheart (*shrieking and rising*) It can't be!

Mrs Fubbs Can't it?

Mrs Goodheart Fifty years ago to this very day *my* father went to see the fair on Clapham Common with *my* sister, and they neither of 'em never come back! And 'er name was—Phoebe!

Mrs Fubbs (*rising*) Oo, I say!

Mrs Goodheart Mrs Fubbs—I am Eliza!

Mrs Fubbs (*trying to remember*) Eliza? . . . Eliza? . . . 'ere, that rings a b—*Eliza*!!!

Mrs Goodheart Phoebe!

They embrace C. *Mrs Goodheart reacts to Mrs Fubbs' gin-sodden breath*

Fancy us bein' neighbours all these years and not knowin'!

Prudence enters L

Prudence Mama dear, here is Dr Probity to see you.

FANFARE

Fanfare. The Lights come up to full

Dr Probity enters L *with her bag, crosses below Prudence and stands, posed,* LC

Probity Good afternoon! And which of these ladies is m'patient?

Mrs Fubbs This one, Doctor. (*Indicating Mrs Goodheart*)

Probity Ah! (*Moving to Mrs Goodheart*)

Mrs Fubbs (*proudly, moving* DR) My sister!

Prudence (*in to* LC) Your sister!

Dr Probity puts her bag on the table and pushes Mrs Goodheart into the chair R *of the table*

Probity Sit down, please . . . and what seems to be the trouble, eh?

Mrs Goodheart 'Ere! I'm not 'avin' no woman doctorin' me!

Probity I assure you, Mrs—? (*She looks at Prudence interrogatively*)

Prudence Goodheart, Doctor.

Probity Mrs Goodheart, that I have a British licence to practise medicine, than which there is none more respected in the whole civilized world!

Mrs Fubbs 'Ear, 'ear!

Mrs Goodheart But——
Probity Put your tongue out, please.

Mrs Goodheart does so while still protesting incoherently. Dr Probity looks at Mrs Goodheart's tongue and then takes her pulse under the following

Prudence Mrs Fubbs, are you really and truly my dear Mama's long-lost elder sister?
Mrs Fubbs That's right, dearie! (*Moving in to Prudence's right*) I'm your Auntie Phoebe!

They embrace and Prudence reacts to Mrs Fubbs' breath

Probity (*cheerfully*) There is nothing wrong with you, Mrs Goodheart, other than strain, exhaustion, malnutrition, the flux, the gripes, and a mild attack of cholera. (*Taking a bottle of medicine from her bag and putting it on the table*) I'll give you a tonic—take that and a couple of weeks in bed and in no time you'll be tickety-boo!
Mrs Goodheart A fortnight in bed? But what about me washin'?
Prudence (*circling round to her right*) Mama dear, you must do as the doctor says—Dr Probity is a very eminent medical luminary!
Probity (*laughing modestly*) What makes you say that, girl?
Prudence I remember now where I've seen your name, Dr Probity—in the newspapers when you attended (*in awed tones*) at Windsor Castle!

MUSIC
✳

Mrs Goodheart rises as music plays two bars of National Anthem allegro, then sits again

Probity (*with a hearty, ringing laugh*) No, Miss Goodheart, that was m'guardian, Sir Trueman Probity, in whose footsteps I am endeavouring to follow, albeit unworthily.
Mrs Fubbs Guardian? Are you a h'orphaning as well, Doctor?
Probity Alas, Mrs—? (*Again she looks at Prudence interrogatively*)
Prudence Fubbs, Doctor.
Probity Mrs Fubbs . . . (*crossing to her*) . . . when but a mere tot, twenty-five years ago to this very day as it happens, m'father was, so they told me, run over in Hyde Park by a carriage and pair.

All react

In the confusion I was left behind, to be placed in a home for foundlings. From there I was rescued by the great Christian gentleman and physician to whom I have just alluded, and brought up as his own. I determined to repay his charitableness by adopting, however humbly, his own noble profession and to devote my life to succouring the poor and needy — like yourselves.

Mrs Fubbs (*to the audience*) Don't she talk nice?

Mrs Goodheart So you never knew 'oo you really was?

Probity The only clue to my origins is a rag-doll that was apparently in my possession at the time, and from which I refused to be parted.

Mrs Goodheart (*trembling*) A rag-doll?!

Probity I have it still; it occupies a place of honour in my boudoir at Probity Grange, Sydenham (*or local reference. She points out front, and then, realizing her orientation is wrong, points in the correct direction*) Upon the hem of its rough gown is embroidered — somewhat crudely, I must allow — the legend: "Property of Matilda".

Mrs Goodheart It's 'er! It's 'er! (*To Prudence*) I never could embroider, could I?

Probity Why this untoward reaction to my unhappy tale?

Prudence (*crossing to Probity's right*) Dr Probity, it would seem that my mother . . . is your mother . . . and that consequently you are my——

Probity Sister!

They embrace. Music, building up to Lady Audley's entrance

Mrs Goodheart Tillie! Oh, my Tillie! (*She opens her arms*)

Probity (*crossing to her*) Mother!

They embrace

Mrs Fubbs (*with arms open*) Niece!

Probity (*with less enthusiasm*) Aunt! (*She crosses and embraces Mrs Fubbs* DLC, *reacting to her breath*)

Prudence and Mrs Goodheart also embrace during this

  Lady Audley enters

Lady Audley Well, Goodheart?

Mrs Fubbs Oo, I say!

Rachmaninov "Prelude". Thunder and lightning. All embraces are broken

Lady Audley (*still at the entrance* L) Do you have my rent?
Mrs Goodheart Oh, well, to tell you the truth—
Probity One moment . . . Mother . . .

Mrs Goodheart giggles coyly and hugs Prudence

Lady Audley (*disconcerted. Out front*) Mother?
Probity Who is this—person?
Lady Audley (*outraged*) Person!?
Prudence This is Lady Audley, Doct—(*blushing prettily*)—Matilda
 . . . who has come for the sadly overdue rent.
Lady Audley Quite so. (*Crossing to* DR) And do you have it . . . or
 not?
Mrs Goodheart I—er—I—
Probity One further moment. Lady Audley, did you say, er—?
 (*Looking at Prudence interrogatively*)
Prudence (*softly*) Prudence, Matilda.
Probity (*also tenderly*) Prudence . . . what a pretty name . . .
 (*Briskly, crossing to Lady Audley*) I'm sure I have seen Lady
 Audley before . . .
Lady Audley I should think that most unlikely.
Probity I have it! Four years ago—in the dock at the Old Bailey!

All react

 You were not Lady Audley then, but—Mrs Vile!

All react

Lady Audley (*at bay*) I was acquitted!
Mrs Goodheart (*coming* DC) Mrs Vile? Wot—'er wot was done for
 poisonin' 'er 'usband's cocoa with strychnine?
Probity The same. I was a student at the time and m'guardian
 thought it would be instructive for me in the field of medical
 jurisprudence to attend the trial. And as I recall, Lady Audley,
 you were exceeding fortunate to escape the rope!
Mrs Fubbs (*sitting on the chair below* L *entrance*) So *that's* Lady
 Audley's secret!
Lady Audley The jury found me not guilty!
Probity (*smiling grimly*) Were women permitted to sit as jurors, the
 verdict had been different! For it was rumoured that to find in

your favour some of those twelve "good men and true" were offered certain . . . inducements . . . of a nature too indelicate to specify in the presence of my maiden sister.

Mrs Goodheart Brazen 'ussy!

Probity And what is more, as I now further recall, Lady Audley had once before been arraigned upon a criminal charge—of manslaughter!

All react

Lady Audley Remorseless!

Probity (*crossing* DL) Yes, twenty-five years ago to this very day, if memory serves me——

All react

—Lady Audley—or Elsie Sproat as she then was——

Mrs Fubbs (*cackling*) Brussel Sproat!

All giggle and snigger. Lady Audley hangs her head in shame

Probity —ran down an innocent bystander in Rotten Row because of her culpable carelessness in handling the reins of her carriage and . . . (*realizing the implication*) . . . of her *carriage and pair*!

Prudence Twenty-five years ago today? Mama—could that innocent bystander have been Papa?

Mrs Goodheart (*to Lady Audley's side*) It was you! You ran over my Charlie!

Probity Of course! Why did I not realize it sooner! The victim was my own father!

Mrs Goodheart And 'e was such an upstandin' man . . .!

Lady Audley (*panicking and crossing to Dr Probity*) I was only a slip of a girl—and I was acquitted!

Probity You were indeed. An unfortunate aberration of our English legal system which nevertheless with all its faults is still the finest in the world!

Mrs Fubbs (*rising*) 'Ear, ear! (*Sitting*)

Prudence (DC) But—Matilda—why should Lady Audley wish to murder her first husband?

Probity (*moving* DR) Sit down and I'll explain. When Mrs Vile first met Lord Audley——

During this speech Lady Audley takes the chair L of the table and stands UL, leaning on the back of the reversed chair as though in the dock. Mrs Fubbs takes her chair and moves to the table C; Prudence takes the chair from R of the table and sits next to Mrs Fubbs; Mrs Goodheart takes the chair from below the R entrance and places it R of Prudence. She angles the table behind the three chairs and then sits. Mrs Goodheart, Prudence and Mrs Fubbs are thus in a line angled against the table between Dr Probity, who is DR, and Lady Audley, who is UL; they turn their heads from side to side as though at a tennis match during the ensuing dialogue. The lighting can change to enhance the inquisitorial atmosphere

—in circumstances shrouded in dubiety, she purported to be a free woman. The misguided Marquis, captivated by her forwardness and sinister charm, offered his hand in marriage. I put it to you, Lady Audley——

Heads turn from Dr Probity to Lady Audley

—that the unfortunate Mr Vile was the only obstacle between you and a Marchioness's coronet; ergo, he had to be eliminated!
Lady Audley It's all lies! Lies, I tell you!

Heads turn back to Dr Probity

Probity For Mr Vile was a poor man, a mere pheasant-plucker from Feltham (*or local reference*), and not to be compared as a matrimonial catch with a noble Marquis!

Heads turn to Lady Audley

Lady Audley Implacable!

Heads turn back to Dr Probity

Probity Not that transgressions of the law were unknown to your family, were they, Lady Audley? I put it to you that your own father was a convicted felon!

Heads turn to Lady Audley

Lady Audley No! Not that!

Heads turn eagerly to Dr Probity

Probity Is it not a fact that your father served a sentence of six years at a treadmill for running over and killing a man, fifty years ago to this very day, while drunk in charge of a Clapham Omnibus!

Lady Audley Mercy!

Mrs Goodheart and Mrs Fubbs are gazing open-mouthed at Dr Probity. Mrs Goodheart, who is on the right of the line, turns and looks at Mrs Fubbs, then looks again at Dr Probity

Mrs Goodheart } *(together)* Not a number forty-two?
Mrs Fubbs

Lady Audley *(involuntarily)* How did you know? (*She claps a hand over her mouth*)

Mrs Fubbs Now there's a coincidence for you, Eliza!

Mrs Goodheart I can't follow any of this . . . Oh, Lor' . . .! (*She looks faint*)

Prudence Have some water, Mama dear. (*She rises and gets the cup from the table behind her*)

The Lights revert to normal

Mrs Fubbs No, don't give 'er none o' that, Pru. It tastes funny.

Probity "Funny", did you say, Aunt? (*She crosses and takes the cup from Prudence, inserts a finger and licks it*) Hmmm . . . (*She returns the cup to Prudence*)

Prudence replaces the cup on the table and again sits c

I saw someone at the well earlier when I came across from number five. It was you, Lady Audley. You had a bottle in your hand; I thought then that you were filling it, but now I realize that you were—(*she snatches Lady Audley's bag from her hand and removes a green poison bottle*)—emptying it! (*She opens the bottle and sniffs the contents*)

Mrs Goodheart What's she been up to now?

Probity Just as I suspected—strychnine!

All react

Mrs Fubbs Oo, I say! We could all 'ave been poisoned in our beds!

Mrs Goodheart No wonder we've all been queer!

Lady Audley *(breaking down)* All right, I confess! I confess! There—are you satisfied?!

Probity *(crossing to Lady Audley's right)* I have no wish to condemn you, unhappy creature, steeped in villainy though you be. (*Out front*) For remember: no-one is wholly bad. And as m'guardian has always enjoined me, I shall be merciful. (*She

gives back the bag, having replaced the bottle) Here, take back the
evidence of your latest malfeasance!

Mrs Fubbs 'Er what?

Lady Audley (*brokenly*) Oh, thank you! Thank you!

Probity (*crossing* DR) All debts accruing from this household are
cancelled?

Lady Audley Yes, yes, they are!

Probity I am content. Come, mother — sister — aunt — let us to the
green fields and salubrious air of Sydenham (*or local reference.
Again she points out front and then in the correct direction*), and to
the comforts of the Grange, where no longer will you suffer want
or hunger. M'guardian will, I know, welcome you and take you
all most warmly to his heart and home!

Mrs Fubbs (*matter-of-factly*) That sounds nice, dear.

Mrs Goodheart Yes, make a nice change, any'ow.

Probity (*out front*) For Justice and Virtue now triumph.

Prudence (*rising and coming down level with Dr Probity*) Let us bless
this happy day!

Mrs Goodheart (*also coming down*) But 'o's goin' to do all me
washin'?

Probity Elsie Sproat?

Lady Audley (*resignedly*) If I must.

Mrs Fubbs (*coming down*) Oo, I say!

*All move into a line downstage except Lady Audley who moves to
above the table and begins sorting out the washing. Chords to
punctuate the final quatrain*

Probity
Prudence } (*together*) Yes, Evil must ever be thwarted,

Mrs Fubbs
Mrs Goodheart } (*together*) Retribution is even now beckoning;

The line opens at the centre to reveal Lady Audley. All look at her

Lady Audley The pleasures of Sin have I courted,

The line closes up again. All look out front

All And today is the day of reckoning!

Black-out or quick curtain

1st picture: *Prudence and Dr Probity are embracing fondly* R, *Mrs Fubbs and Mrs Goodheart embracing* L. *Lady Audley is above the table looking tragic with back of her hand to her brow*

2nd picture: *Mrs Fubbs and Prudence are now embracing* R, *Mrs Goodheart and Dr Probity* L. *Lady Audley is looking in horror at some soiled and unspeakable garment*

Then a straight line-up and curtsys. Snappy music throughout all pictures and calls

FURNITURE AND PROPERTY LIST

Drapes are quite sufficient; if available a humble kitchen set may be used, painted in a broad, highly coloured pantomime style.

On stage: Table
4 chairs

Off-stage: Large bundle of washing done up in a sheet and containing a
soiled garment **(Mrs Goodheart)**
Study books **(Prudence)**
Cup **(Mrs Fubbs)**
Gladstone bag. *In it:* bottle of tonic **(Dr Probity)**

Personal: **Mrs Fubbs:** small bottle of gin in pocket
Lady Audley: evening bag containing small green fluted poison
bottle; lorgnette (optional)
Dr Probity: nurse's watch

LIGHTING PLOT

A kitchen. Interior

To open: General lighting, not quite full up

Cue 1	**Mrs Fubbs:** "Oo, I say!" *Lighning (blue or red flashes)*	(Page 75)
Cue 2	**Lady Audley:** "Remember—one hour!" (*She exits* R) *Lightning*	(Page 76)
Cue 3	**Mrs Goodheart:** ". . . if only 'e was 'ere now! If only . . ." *Snap check down. Green spot on Mrs Goodheart*	(Page 77)
Cue 4	As **Mrs Goodheart** throws her apron over her face *Restore lighting to previous level*	(Page 77)
Cue 5	**Prudence:** ". . . here is Dr Probity to see you." *Fade up to full*	(Page 79)
Cue 6	**Mrs Fubbs:** "Oo, I say!" *Lightning*	(Page 81)
Cue 7	As cast get into position for "courtroom" sequence *Check down*	(Page 84)
Cue 8	**Prudence:** "Have some water, Mama dear." *Restore lighting to previous level*	(Page 85)
Cue 9	**All:** "And today is the day of reckoning!" *Black-out*	(Page 86)

Full up and down as required for pictures

EFFECTS PLOT

COSTUMES

Mrs Goodheart: Nondescript full-length dress or blouse and skirt in dull colours. Apron. Black or brown boots. Mob-cap.

Prudence Goodheart: Pretty but simple day-dress or blouse and skirt. Ribbons in hair. Matching shoes. No gloves.

Mrs Fubbs: As for Mrs Goodheart but without apron and mob-cap. She could wear a shawl, mittens and a battered hat.

Lady Audley: Full evening-dress with bare shoulders, preferably scarlet with perhaps a cloak. Elbow-length gloves. Feathers or a tiara in her hair. Lots of glittering jewellery.

Dr Probity: Very smart two-piece suit with matching hat. No gloves.

MAKE-UP

Mrs Goodheart: Washed-out base, untidy hair, perhaps spectacles. Big bosom.

Prudence Goodheart: Straight juvenile, no false eyelashes or coloured nail-polish. Ringlets or hair loose.

Mrs Fubbs: As for Mrs Goodheart. Can wear spectacles if Mrs Goodheart does not. Perhaps some blacked-out teeth.

Lady Audley: Very glamorous and dramatic. Heavy false eye-lashes. Pale base with lots of rouge and eye-shadow. Hair up.

Dr Probity: Straight. No false eye-lashes. Keep the eyes clear. Hair in a bun or a piece.

MADE AND PRINTED IN GREAT BRITAIN BY
LATIMER TREND & COMPANY LTD PLYMOUTH
MADE IN ENGLAND